110 Amazing Apps for Education

Author

Rane Anderson

SHELL EDUCATION

Publishing Credits

Dona Herweck Rice, *Editor-in-Chief*; Robin Erickson, *Production Director*; Lee Aucoin, *Creative Director*; Timothy J. Bradley, *Illustration Manager*; Kristy Stark, M.A.Ed., *Senior Editor*; James Anderson, *Editor*; Grace Alba, *Print Designer*; Scott Laumann, Don Tran, *Production Designers*; Corinne Burton, M.A.Ed., *Publisher*

Shell Education

5301 Oceanus Drive
Huntington Beach, CA 92649-1030
http://www.shelleducation.com
ISBN 978-1-4258-0847-1

© 2012 Shell Educational Publishing, Inc.
Reprinted 2013

The opinions, descriptions, and ideas presented in this book do not reflect the opinions or ideas of any of the app developers mentioned. The app developers mentioned within in no way endorse this book or Shell Education. All information presented is accurate as of the date of publication. Some of the apps presented in this book are free but a majority are for purchase. The classroom teacher or parent may reproduce copies of materials in this book for educational use only. The reproduction of any part for an entire school or school system is strictly prohibited. No part of this publication may be transmitted, stored, or recorded in any form without written permission from the publisher.

Table of Contents

Table of Contents *(cont.)*

#50847—110 Amazing Apps for Education

© Shell Education

Introduction

Dear Parents and Educators,

The world is changing quickly. Each day we move closer to a true global community, held together by ideas, technology, and collaboration. In this competitive global community, the need to empower children with specialized twenty-first century skills becomes increasingly evident. In turn, this has led many schools to invest heavily in technology to keep children competitive in the future global job market.

Children born into this global community think and learn differently than their parents and grandparents did. They are constantly surrounded by digital mediums, all vying for their attention. As a parent and educator, it is important to consider what types of technology—and more importantly, what types of information—we present to our children. And because we compete with so much additional stimuli, it is vital to choose carefully the most effective and concise tools to use, as well as the best practices in which to present knowledge. This book has been written with all of this in mind.

110 Amazing Apps for Education provides parents and educators the opportunity to quickly locate curriculum-based apps that are perfect and worthwhile for classroom or home use. The apps chosen have been specifically culled to help children master twenty-first century skills, as well as to sharpen their skills across the academic curriculum. Specific suggestions are offered for using the apps in the classroom and at home. And every app presented is fun, engaging, and sure to increase student knowledge and skills. Best of all, you as a parent or educator are sure to enjoy them, too!

With best wishes for your success,

James Anderson, M.S.Ed.
Technology Editor

How to Use This Book

A Word About Apps

Incorporating technology into homes and classrooms is easier than it has ever been. With just a tap of a finger, you can unlock a whole world of educational information from which your children and students will benefit. For teachers, this means having the information you need to supplement a lesson within seconds. For parents, this means making sure your child gets the most out of his or her education, even at home. The apps in this book have been carefully chosen to meet your child's educational needs.

How to Purchase and Download an App

Purchase and download an app on a computer or directly on a mobile device (tablet or phone).

On a Computer

Apps are available for purchase from the iTunes® store for Apple® and Google Play and the Amazon™ Appstore for Android.

Example Using iTunes

1 Open iTunes, and select the iTunes store.

2 Place the cursor into the search field and type in an app title or developer name.

3 Find the iPad section in the search results and click the **see all** link.

4 Find the app you would like to download and click the button to download.

Note: To purchase Android™ Apps from Google Play or the Amazon™ Appstore for Android, visit:

- Google Play: http://play.google.com
- Amazon Appstore: http://www.amazon.com

How to Use This Book

From Your Mobile Device

Each mobile device (tablet or phone) includes a built-in app for purchasing and downloading apps.

Example Using an iPad or iPhone

1 Tap the App Store icon. (**Note:** Your device must be connected to the internet to browse the App Store.)

2 type the title of the app in the search field to locate the app by title.

3 Find the iPad section in the search results and tap the **see all** link.

4 Select the app you wish to purchase

5 Click on the price beneath the icon to purchase the app.

The app is now ready to use. Scroll through the home screen to locate the app.

How to Use This Book

How to Connect to the Internet

An app may require you to connect your mobile device to the Internet to use it.

Example Using an iPad or iPhone

1 Tap the Settings icon on the home screen.

2 Select the Wi-Fi tab.

3 Make sure Wi-Fi is turned on and that your network is selected.

4 To connect to your network, find the network name. Tap on it, and enter the network password.

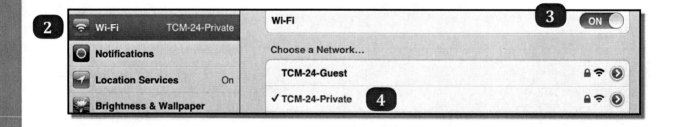

How to Use This Book

How to Locate Additional Settings for Apps

Some apps allow you to change settings from within the app itself. Other apps allow you to change additional settings from the Settings menu on your device.

Example Using an iPad or iPhone

1 Tap the Settings icon on the home screen.

2 Scroll through the list of apps and select an app to review its settings.

3 A list of settings for that app will appear. Adjust the settings to fit your learning needs.

All changes will be applied to the app as you exit the Settings menu by clicking the home button.

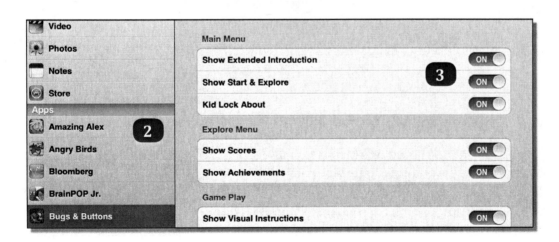

How to Use This Book

Every app page includes an image of the app icon, the title of the app, the company name, and the suggested grade range. Use this information to find the app in an app store.

A description is provided for every app, including key features.

The At School and At Home sections provided focused examples of how each app can be used at home and in the classroom in the appropriate curriculum area.

ABC Animals
Critical Matter, Inc.

Suggested Grades
Pre-K–K

Available
iTunes, Amazon

Description

ABC Animals is an interactive flash card app that will motivate children to recognize, say, and write the letters of the alphabet. Listen to the name of the letter and animal. Then, double tap the card to flip it over and practice writing the letter. Shake your device to erase and write the letter again. *ABC Animals* includes the following key features:

> Letter cards that include uppercase and lowercase letters along with an illustration
> Card Randomizer
> Choice of D'Nealian or Zaner-Bloser handwriting methods
> Alphabet practice in English, French, German, or Spanish

Note: Features can be adjusted from your mobile device's Settings menu.

At School

> In pairs, instruct students to say each letter and animal displayed. Then, have students practice writing letters on the back of each card. Arrows and dotted lines are available to help students write each letter correctly. Demonstrate how to carefully share the mobile device so that students may take turns writing.
> In teacher-led small groups, help students write each letter. Monitor that they are making the correct stroke marks, in the right order.
> In a whole-group instructional setting, connect your mobile device to a projector. Display the flash cards, and practice saying the letters and animal names as a group. Demonstrate how to write each letter using the mobile device, and ask for volunteers to write letters in front of the class.

At Home

> Disable the audio for the app. Flip through each flash card. As you do, have your child point to each letter and animal and say the name of each aloud.
> Encourage your child to write on the back of the flash card using the arrows or dotted line guides. Then, have him or her practice without the guides.
> After using *ABC Animals*, work with your child to spot the letters in favorite books and even on signs and buildings in the world around you.

Projecting Your Apps in the Classroom

For many of the apps presented in this book, it is beneficial to project the screen of your mobile device for all students in a classroom to view. Many mobile devices have an adapter for purchase that will allow you to directly connect it to a projector. If an adapter is not available, placing your mobile device under a document camera will provide a similar result. Some mobile devices and projectors allow wireless connections as well. Choose the method that is most appropriate for you.

How I Use My Apps Pages

A page has been provided at the beginning of each section to allow you to take notes about the apps you are using. Use this page to note additional lesson ideas and reflections. Or, list other useful apps that could compliment those provided in each section of this book.

Amazing Language Arts Apps

How I Use My Apps

ABC Animals
Critical Matter, Inc.

Suggested Grades
Pre-K–K

Available
iTunes, Amazon

Description

ABC Animals is an interactive flash card app that will motivate children to recognize, say, and write the letters of the alphabet. Listen to the name of the letter and animal. Then, double tap the card to flip it over and practice writing the letter. Shake your device to erase and write the letter again. *ABC Animals* includes the following key features:

> Letter cards that include uppercase and lowercase letters along with an illustration

> Card Randomizer

> Choice of D'Nealian or Zaner-Bloser handwriting methods

> Alphabet practice in English, French, German, or Spanish

Note: Features can be adjusted from your mobile device's Settings menu.

At School

> In pairs, instruct students to say each letter and animal displayed. Then, have students practice writing letters on the back of each card. Arrows and dotted lines are available to help students write each letter correctly. Demonstrate how to carefully share the mobile device so that students may take turns writing.

> In teacher-led small groups, help students write each letter. Monitor that they are making the correct stroke marks, in the right order.

> In a whole-group instructional setting, connect your mobile device to a projector. Display the flash cards, and practice saying the letters and animal names as a group. Demonstrate how to write each letter using the mobile device, and ask for volunteers to write letters in front of the class.

At Home

> Disable the audio for the app. Flip through each flash card. As you do, have your child point to each letter and animal and say the name of each aloud.

> Encourage your child to write on the back of the flash card using the arrows or dotted line guides. Then, have him or her practice without the guides.

> After using *ABC Animals*, work with your child to spot the letters in favorite books and even on signs and buildings in the world around you.

Wheels on the Bus

Duck Duck Moose

Suggested Grades
Pre-K–K

Available
iTunes, Google Play, Amazon

Description

Watch this popular children's song come alive with spinning bus wheels, swishing windshield wipers, barking dogs, and more! Kids will love to explore this musical storybook to find the hidden animations. *Itsy Bitsy Spider, Baa Baa Black Sheep,* and *Old Mac Donald* apps are also available from Duck Duck Moose. *Wheels on the Bus* includes the following key features:

> Singing in English, Spanish, French, German, or Italian

> Record function

> Song played in violin, cello, piano, or kazoo

Note: Features can be adjusted from your mobile device's Settings menu.

At School

> In teacher-led small groups, have students record themselves singing the song. Allow students time to play their recorded song to another group or to the class.

> In a whole-group instructional setting, connect your mobile device to a projector. Enable the Auto Turn Pages function in the Settings menu. Point to the words of the song as they are sung. Teach students hand motions to match the lyrics. Encourage them to sing the lyrics that they know.

> As an extension, have students design a new page for the app. Have them create a new verse for the song, draw what the new page would look like, and describe one or two animations that could make their new page more engaging.

At Home

> Teach your child how to navigate the app. Tap various objects on the screen to demonstrate how to find hidden animations.

> Allow your child to listen to the song played with different instruments.

> Ask your child to help you record your own version of the song. Encourage him or her to sing with you. Play the recording for other family members.

> After using *Wheels on the Bus*, work with your child to create additional lyrics to the song. Have your child sing the new lyrics.

© Shell Education

Speech with Milo: Prepositions

Doonan Speech Therapy, Inc.

Suggested Grades
Pre-K–1

Available
iTunes

Description

The adorable mouse Milo is eager to help teach prepositions, such as *above*, *below*, and *across*, along with 20 others. Unlike basic flash cards, this app uses fun animations to keep children interested while learning. *Speech with Milo: Verbs, Interactive Storybook, and Sequencing* apps are also available from Doonan Speech Therapy, Inc. *Speech with Milo: Prepositions* includes the following key features:

❯ Option to activate or deselect words from the word pool

❯ Option to show words in random order

❯ Background music on/off switch

At School

❯ Place this app in a center and allow students to practice at least five prepositions with Milo.

❯ In pairs, instruct students to take turns saying preposition opposites. For example, if one student says, "over," the other student should reply, "under."

❯ In teacher-led small groups, have students answer *Where* questions. Have them explain where Milo is and how he got there.

❯ In a whole-group instructional setting, connect your mobile device to a projector. Adjust the app settings to select the prepositions you would like to teach. Display a preposition activity page. Allow students to hear the phrase. Divide the class into groups and have students act out the phrase.

At Home

❯ Allow your child to listen to the preposition and prepositional phrase. Then, help him or her come up with an additional sentence using that preposition.

❯ Encourage your child to say the preposition with the recording. Have him or her repeat the prepositional phrase.

❯ Help your child create hand motions to go along with each word or phrase.

❯ After using *Speech with Milo: Prepositions*, work with your child to use prepositions to describe the world around you.

Richard Scarry's Busytown

Night & Day Studios, Inc.

Suggested Grades
Pre-K–2

Available
iTunes

Description

Richard Scarry's imaginative best-selling series is now an interactive picture book. Begin your adventure by choosing a character, picking its name, and dressing it up. Then, explore different rooms of a house and around town. Search for objects in each room. And, do not forget about Goldbug. He is hidden, and you have to find him! *Richard Scarry's Busytown* includes the following key features:

> Animations that come to life with a tap

> New missions for every room

> Six interactive rooms

> Option to save game

> Audio feedback

At School

> Place this app in a center and allow students to search for objects.

> In pairs, instruct students to take turns searching for objects. Have students send each other on missions. For example, one student can ask the other, "Where is the turnip?" or "Where is the toothpaste?"

> In teacher-led small groups, have students look for objects together. When the object is found, write the word on a small whiteboard, and allow students to spell out the word while they write it on their whiteboards.

> After using *Richard Scarry's Busytown*, turn your classroom into a Busytown room. Attach labels to objects. Send students on missions to find objects.

At Home

> Help your child create a character and search for Busytown objects.

> Say each object's name with your child as he or she taps the picture.

> After using *Richard Scarry's Busytown*, have your child to spot objects around you. Ask your child to help you figure out the letters that spell the name of each object he or she finds. Sound out each word, and write the words for him or her to read.

     © Shell Education

Hickory Dickory Dock

Mindshapes Limited

Suggested Grades
Pre-K–2

Available
iTunes

Description

Learn the numbers on an analog clock face and view the clock hands at each hour with this classic nursery rhyme as a fun backdrop. The built-in visual and audio cues will help children learn numbers 1–12, while the playful mouse will keep them entertained with humorous animations and interactive games. *Hickory Dickory Dock* includes the following key features:

> Lyrics to the nursery rhyme

> Visual and audio cues

> Interactive mini-games

> Engaging sound effects and graphics

At School

> Place this app in a center and allow students to become familiar with the numbers on a clock face.

> In pairs, instruct students to take turns first setting the time on the clock and then playing the mini-game that follows. Encourage students to work together if they are having trouble.

> In teacher-led small groups, use a practice clock to review the numbers on a clock face and the placement of the hour hand. Have students move the hour hand to different times. Then, allow them to practice the same concept using the *Hickory Dickory Dock* app.

At Home

> Show your child how to set the time on the clock in the *Hickory Dickory Dock* app. Explain that after the time is set correctly, a mini game will appear.

> After using *Hickory Dickory Dock*, work with your child to recognize the numbers on an analog clock at home. Ask questions such as "What number is the hour hand on now?" and "We are eating dinner one hour from now. What number will the hour hand be on in one hour?" and so on.

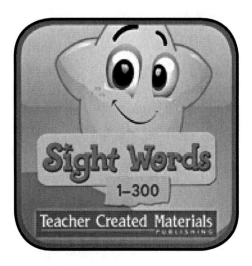

Kids Learn Sight Words: 1–300

Teacher Created Materials, Inc.

Suggested Grades
Pre-K–3 and emerging readers of all ages

Available
iTunes

Description

Kids Learn Sight Words: 1–300 is not just another flash card sight word app. It is an interactive, engaging, and fun app that allows emerging readers of all ages to practice speaking, reading, and writing sight words. *Kids Learn Sight Words: 1–300* includes the following key features:

> Audio for each word and Record and Playback functions

> Finger-activated writing

> Shake eraser

> Choice from your mobile device's Settings menu to save or clear students' work upon closing the app.

> Mini-games, such as word search, concentration, and hangman

At School

> Place this app in a center and allow students to build their sight word fluency.

> In pairs, instruct students to take turns writing sight words and recording them.

> In teacher-led small groups, have students take turns reading and recording the sight words. Then have students work in pairs to create and read sentences and play the sight word mini-games.

> In a whole-group instructional setting, connect your mobile device to a projector. Display a sight word and ask for a volunteer to read it aloud. Ask the class to repeat the sight word while you record it. Then, play it back to them.

At Home

> Encourage your child to say a word and then touch it to have it read aloud.

> Have your child practice using the sight words in sentences.

> Help your child play and master the sight word mini-games. Then, have him or her create their own game using the sight words.

> After using *Kids Learn Sight Words: 1–300*, work with your child to spot the sight words in favorite books and on signs and buildings in the world around you.

PopOut! The Tale of Peter Rabbit

Loud Crow Interactive Inc.

Suggested Grades
Pre-K–4

Available
iTunes, Google Play, Amazon

Description

Beatrix Potter's classic tale of the mischievous Peter Rabbit has been remastered in this charming interactive storybook app. Beautiful illustrations come to life as you read or listen along. Interact with the engaging animations that will enchant readers of all ages! *PopOut! The Tale of Peter Rabbit* includes the following key features:

> Pull-down menu for page selection

> Each word spoken when tapped

> Highlights words in sync with recording

> Page turning with the flick of a finger

> Fun sound effects and relaxing music

At School

> Place this app in a center and allow students to read *PopOut! The Tale of Peter Rabbit*.

> In pairs, instruct students to take turns reading pages. Have students write character descriptions as they read. When they have finished, instruct students to write about their favorite scenes from the story.

> In a whole-group instructional setting, connect your mobile device to a projector. Have students listen to *PopOut! The Tale of Peter Rabbit*. Then, divide the class into groups. Have students create paper puppets to represent the characters in the story. Allow students time to design a puppet show to perform in front of the class.

At Home

> Read *PopOut! The Tale of Peter Rabbit* with your child. Ask him or her *Who*, *What*, *When*, *Where*, and *Why* questions to build comprehension skills. For example, ask questions such as "Why does Mrs. Rabbit warn Flopsy, Mopsy, Cotton-tail, and Peter to stay out of Mr. McGregor's garden?"

> Select the Read Myself option before beginning. Encourage your child to read the story aloud with you. Help him or her sound out difficult words.

Cinderella

Nosy Crow Limited

Suggested Grades
Pre-K–4

Available
iTunes

Description

The joy of reading the timeless tale of Cinderella is enhanced with the added fun of interacting with the characters.   Touch the characters and they speak. Tap or slide the screen for hidden animations in important scenes. Help Cinderella complete tasks such as cleaning up after her stepsisters. *Cinderella* includes the following key features:

> Colorful illustrations and engaging characters

> Narrator's words at the bottom of the screen

> Option to change the length of time in which text appears on the screen

> Three modes for reading: Read to Me, Read by Myself, and Read and Play

At School

> In a whole-group instructional setting, connect your mobile device to a projector. Read the story with the class and ask for volunteers to help you explore each scene for moveable objects and animations.

> In pairs, have students read the story together. Instruct them to take turns reading the narration and the dialogue.

> After reading *Cinderella*, have younger students create a skit to reenact the Cinderella story. Encourage them to add their own twist to the story. Allow students time before their performance to create stage props and backdrops.

> Have older students highlight one of the characters from the story by writing a short narrative featuring that character.

At Home

> Read the story together with your child. Ask your child which character and which part of the story is his or her favorite and why.

> Have your child draw a picture of a favorite character, showing what he or she does after this story ends. Help your child write a paragraph to describe what happens.

> Assist your child in creating a diorama of his or her favorite scene from the story. Have him or her include a title and write a brief description of the scene that includes the setting and the characters involved.

© Shell Education

iWriteWords

gdiplus

Suggested Grades
K–1

Available
iTunes

Description

Drag Mr. Crab across the screen to help him collect the numbers while writing letters and words. See a cute drawing appear when you are finished! Then glide each letter into the rotating star to complete the level. Don't forget to sing along with the interactive *ABC* song sheet music! *iWriteWords* includes the following key features:

> 70 word levels, 20 number levels, 26 levels using uppercase letters, and 26 levels using lowercase letters

> Option to record and play screencasts of your child's handwriting

> Writing practice for letters, words, and numbers

> Choice of two handwriting styles

Note: Features can be adjusted from your mobile device's Settings menu.

At School

> Have younger students practice writing numbers, and uppercase and lowercase letters. Then, instruct them to practice the beginning word levels. Make sure the difficulty setting is set to Easy.

> Have older students start with the beginning word levels. Consider changing the difficulty level for these students from Easy to Medium or Hard.

> In a whole-group instructional setting, connect your mobile device to a projector. Display the *ABC* song sheet music. Invite a student to be the ABC "musician" and tap the musical notes to make the music play. Have the class sing along with the music.

At Home

> Work with your child to practice writing letters and numbers by dragging the crab.

> Sing the *ABC* song to your child while he or she taps the sheet music. Make the activity a game by having your child change the song's tempo (by tapping faster or slower).

> Encourage your child to practice writing letters, numbers, and words of increasing difficulty. Change the difficulty level in the Settings menu as needed.

Smarty Pants School

Smarty Pants School LLC

Suggested Grades
K–2

Available
iTunes

Description

Smarty Pants School is a fun way to get children pumped about learning! It begins by evaluating a child's aptitude in letter knowledge, phonemic awareness, phonics, regular phonetic words, and irregular sight words. Then, it places a child into the appropriate class that will strengthen early reading skills. *Smarty Pants School* includes the following key features:

> Five classes, each focusing on a particular reading skill

> Activities suited for English language and special needs learners

> Engaging games, activities, and puzzles in each class of increasing difficulty

> Tracking for multiple children's progress

> Presents a colorful diploma that can be printed or emailed to family and friends

At School

> Have students work independently to complete the app's assessment.

> In small homogeneous groups, have students work together to strengthen their early reading skills. Instruct them to give one another support as each student completes a level.

> In a whole-group instructional setting, connect your mobile device to a projector. Display an activity that will supplement the concepts you are currently teaching or that will help review concepts you have already taught. Help students graduate each class level. Award your class with a diploma after they've achieved success.

At Home

> Have your child complete the app's assessment. Work closely with him or her to offer pointers and encouragement when completing each class.

> Allow your child to show you his or her favorite games, activities, or puzzles. Encourage him or her to complete an activity while you watch, and offer praise after a job well done.

> If your child is guessing before selecting answers, model a few activities for him or her. Speak your thought process aloud so your child can use you as a model.

                                        © Shell Education

Word Wagon

Duck Duck Moose, Partnership

Suggested Grades
K–2

Available
iTunes

Description

Mozzarella the mouse and Coco the bird take you on a playful adventure to learn letters, words, and phonics. First, unscramble the letters on screen to form a word. Then, listen to Mozzarella or Coco sound out each word. Collect the colorful sticker rewards and earn stars to form constellations! *Word Wagon* includes the following key features:

> Over 100 words, including Dolch words

> Illustrations, animations, and sounds for each word

> Seven categories, including animals, food, vehicles, numbers and colors, around the house, and Mozzarella and Coco's favorites

> Four levels of increasing difficulty

At School

> In a whole-group instructional setting, connect your mobile device to a projector. Load *Word Wagon* and tap the flashing **Eiffel Tower** button in the lower-right portion of the screen. Have students watch the introduction story to meet Mozzarella and Coco before they use the app.

> Place this app in a center and have students play a level best suited to their academic needs.

> In teacher-led small groups, have students work together to form words, taking turns to place the letters in the correct order. Have them sound out the words along with the recording. Allow students to take turns picking word categories.

At Home

> Choose a level that is appropriate for your child's academic needs. Choose a word category together. Then, have your child practice forming and sounding out words.

> Review your child's progress by pressing the **Sticker Book** button in the top-left corner of the screen. Have your child tap the stickers to see them come to life!

> Advance to a more difficult level, and work with your child to form words. Switch off placing letters in their correct order. Sound out the word with your child before allowing him or her to drag the letters.

SpellBoard

Palaware

Suggested Grades
K–3

Available
iTunes

Description

Whether on the go or in the middle of a homework session, *SpellBoard* is the perfect addition to your learning toolbox. Enter spelling words from your spelling list, and record your own voice speaking each word. It's that easy! *SpellBoard* can randomize the quiz word order or quiz you from the top of the list to the bottom. *SpellBoard* includes the following key features:

> Option to make spelling lists in multiple languages

> Virtual whiteboard for writing

> Multiple student profiles to track performance (spelling lists can also be shared)

> Word definitions provided by Wordnik

Note: Words and recordings should be entered before starting an activity.

At School

> Place this app in a center and allow students to practice their spelling words.

> In pairs, instruct students to take the quiz. Have them tap the **Speak Word** button to hear the word spoken. Ask students to take turns typing words into the yellow field or writing out the word on the virtual whiteboard at the bottom of the screen.

> In a whole-group instructional setting, use *SpellBoard* to administer the weekly spelling quiz. Make quiz days more fun by having your students record the spelling words in their own voices.

At Home

> Help your child create a spelling list and record his or her voice speaking each word. Then, demonstrate how to randomize the word order of a quiz.

> Ask family members to record the spelling words in their voices to make practicing spelling words and taking the quiz more enjoyable for your child.

> Help your child practice each of his or her weekly spelling words. Challenge your child to learn the definitions of each word, learn other words that are in the same word family, and use each word correctly in a sentence.

    © *Shell Education*

Mad Libs

Penguin Group USA

Suggested Grades
K–6

Available
iTunes

Description

Create the silliest stories ever using *Mad Libs*! All you have to do is fill in the blanks using different parts of speech. Choose from the Story Selection screen and get started. Use the **HINTS** button if you get stumped. *Mad Libs* includes the following key features:

> Email option to share stories with friends and family

> Practice with various parts of speech, such as verbs, adjectives, adverbs, nouns, and pronouns

> **HINTS** button gives word examples

At School

> In small groups, have students work together to create *Mad Libs*. Instruct groups to assign one reader and one or more writers. Have the reader enter the words that the writer(s) suggest. When completed, have the reader read the story to the group. Help groups as needed.

> In pairs, instruct students to keep a list of the words they used to fill in the blanks. Then, have them find at least one synonym and one antonym for each word.

> In teacher-led small groups, review the different parts of speech used in *Mad Libs*.

> In a whole-group instructional setting, connect your mobile device to a projector. Have students vote to choose a story. Allow students to contribute words to fill in the blanks. Then, read the completed story to the class.

At Home

> Work with your child to complete a *Mad Libs* story. Encourage him or her to tap the **HINTS** button if needed. Review the different parts of speech you encounter in the story.

> Invite your family to help your child complete a story.

> After using *Mad Libs*, work with your child to create his or her own fill-in-the-blank story. Have your child recruit other family members to fill in the blanks and finish the story.

StoryLines

Root-One Inc.

Suggested Grades
K–12

Available
iTunes

Description

StoryLines is a creative drawing and writing game that begins with a common saying or phrase. That saying is passed to a friend to illustrate. Passed on again, the new illustration gets a title. And what's the end result? You never know what you're going to get! The new title and drawing may not be anything like the original saying or phrase. *StoryLines* includes the following key features:

> Pass-N-Play mode or Facebook™ option

> Choice of a Small, Medium, Large, or Epic *StoryLines*

> Suggestions of famous quotes or sayings

At School

> Place this app in a center and allow students to work together to complete a story line. Have students read their completed story line together.

> Have younger students start a story line for the teacher to finish. Read the completed story line together.

> In a whole-group instructional setting, divide the class into nine groups. Create a new Pass-N-Play story line with nine links. Have students in each group work together to form either a title or an illustration to add to the previous part of the story line. After each group has added either an illustration or title, connect your mobile device to a projector. Play the complete story line for the class to enjoy.

At Home

> Play *StoryLines* with your entire family. For an extra challenge, create a theme each illustrator or title giver must follow. Some examples of themes are *Halloween*, *first day of school*, *Christmas*, *mad scientist*, *Hanukkah*, and *at the beach*. Make sure to pair younger family members with older siblings. Gather together to watch the complete *StoryLine* play out.

Dictionary.com

Dictionary.com, LLC

Suggested Grades

K–12

Available

iTunes, Google Play, Amazon

Description

Dictionary.com is now accessible from your mobile device. And once it's downloaded, you don't even need an Internet connection to search for words! With over 2,000,000 words and definitions included, you'll never be tongue-tied again! *Dictionary.com* includes the following key features:

> Definitions, synonym, and antonym search

> Alphabetical indexing and spelling suggestions

> Word origin and history

> Favorite Word List and Word of the Day

> Voice recognition and audio pronunciation

At School

> Help younger students use the app when learning to spell words, write definitions, and write spelling word sentences.

> Have students participate in Dictionary Day, which falls on October 16th or complete this activity on another day of your choosing. Send students on a word scavenger hunt to learn new words. Add a word or two they are familiar with but of which they may not know the exact meaning.

> Have students use creative writing skills to make up new words for a class dictionary. Instruct them to use the app as a reference and to help with ideas. Suggest that they combine words, shorten words, or modify words that are in the dictionary. Have them work in groups and present their new words to the class.

At Home

> Help your child look up words he or she uses incorrectly or does not understand.

> Send your child on a word quest to help you research a word you want to understand. Have him or her give you one or two synonyms for the word.

> Play a Jeopardy®-style word game with your family. Sort words by topic. Remember, the questions will consist of definitions, and the answers will consist of the matching words.

Analogy

Nth Fusion LLC

Suggested Grades
1–5

Available
iTunes

Description

Sharpen your problem-solving skills with *Analogy*. Your goal is to complete the pattern by analyzing the similarities and differences in a sequence. Then click, or drag and drop the word, picture, or shape that fits the missing space. *Analogy* can help strengthen analytical thinking, perception, spatial skills, memory, and creativity. *Analogy* includes the following key features:

> Options to choose difficulty level, number of questions, and types of analogies

> Rules displayed at the beginning of each session

> Shows correct answer after an incorrect answer is selected

At School

> Place this app in a center and allow students to complete analogies.

> In pairs, instruct students to work together to complete analogies. After becoming proficient in the app, have students create their own analogies on paper. Encourage each pair to present their analogies to another pair to solve.

> In a whole-group instructional setting, connect your mobile device to a projector. Display an analogy for students to complete as a class. Encourage students to explain how they decided which picture, word, or shape completed the pattern.

At Home

> Set the difficulty level to Easy while your child becomes familiar with the app. Then, change the setting to best suit his or her capabilities.

> Have your child justify an answer choice before submitting it. Identify and clarify any misconceptions your child may have. Engage him or her in a conversation about the relationships between the concepts presented.

> Challenge your child to complete as many analogies as possible in three minutes. Keep track of correct and incorrect answers. Encourage your child to try to beat his or her record.

> Have your child explain what an analogy is to a younger child, and have the two work together to complete the patterns.

© Shell Education

Bluster!

McGraw-Hill School Education Group

Suggested Grades
2–4

Available
iTunes

Description

Build vocabulary skills with *Bluster!*, an electrifying word-matching game! Play in Solo, Versus, or Team mode while you race against the weather as you match synonyms, rhyming words, prefixes and suffixes, adjectives, and more. *Bluster!* includes the following key features:

> Activities sorted by grade level and subject matter

> Fun animations and sound effects

> Scoreboard for different playing modes

> Over 800 vocabulary words

At School

> Place this app in a center and allow students to select activities based on grade level, encouraging students to try each match type for their grade level.

> In pairs, have students play in Versus mode to see who can make the most matches first. Or, have them play in Team mode to match words.

> In teacher-led small groups, review the match-type categories. For example, in a second-grade class, you might discuss rhyming words, prefixes, and synonyms. Give multiple examples of each word type to help students play *Bluster!*

> Set up a *Bluster!* tournament. Work with your students to create a tournament bracket, matching students against each other (using the Versus mode) until there are only two students left in the tournament. At this point, connect your mobile device to a projector. Display the final *Bluster!* match for the class to watch.

At Home

> Play in Versus mode with your child. Offer to give him or her a head start.

> If your child masters the match categories for his or her grade level, encourage him or her to try the next grade level. Review the categories, making sure your child understands each match type.

> Work with your child to write a poem using three of the rhyming match words you encountered while playing *Bluster!*

Boggle

Electronic Arts Inc.

Suggested Grades
3–8

Available
iTunes

Description

....

Think you are good with words? Here is your chance to find out! Play the classic *Boggle* word search game, and race against the clock. First, shake the screen to shuffle the 3-D letter cubes.   Then, drag your finger over the letters to form as many words as possible before time runs out. *Boggle* includes the following key features:

> List of all possible words that can be found in each game and their definitions

> Quick Play, Multiplayer, and Advanced modes

At School

....

> Place this app in a center of up to four students to play in Pass 'N Play mode. Students will enter their names and then have three minutes each to find as many words as they can. The student with the highest score wins. Have students work on a vocabulary related assignment while they wait for their turn.

> In a whole-group instructional setting, connect your mobile device to a projector. Write the following point system on the board: 3 and 4 letter words = 1 point; 5 letter words = 2 points; 6 letter words = 3 points; 7 letter words = 5 points; 8+ letter words = 11 points. Shake your mobile device to shuffle the letters to start the three-minute timer. Tell students to write as many words as they can find in the time limit. The student with the highest score wins. Have students check their words against the *Boggle* word list when time is up.

At Home

....

> Work as a team with your child to find words and rack up the points!

> Challenge your child in a Pass 'N Play game to see who can get the highest score.

> At the end of each game, scroll down the list of all the possible words to be found. Have your child find words for which he or she does not know the definition. Then, have your child activate the definition and go over it with him or her.

> Start a *Boggle* tournament at your next family get-together. Challenge participants to find the longest words possible. Give bonus points to players that can accurately tell you the definitions of the words they found.

© Shell Education

Scrabble

Electronic Arts Inc.

Suggested Grades
4–12

Available
iTunes, Google Play, Amazon

Description

Scrabble is the ultimate word game. Form words using the letter tiles, and then drag them onto the virtual 15 × 15 board. Watch the tiles flash as your score is counted! *Scrabble* includes the following key features:

> In-game word list, built-in *Scrabble* dictionary, and best word feature

> Choice of game style, dictionaries, and game difficulty

> Solo vs. Computer, Local Network Play, Pass 'N Play, Party Play, and Play Facebook Friends modes

At School

> In pairs, have students play against each other. Instruct them to keep a list of the words they use during the game. Then, have them write a sentence using each word.

> Facilitate a discussion about anagrams with younger students. Write *one word*, *new door*, and *nor do we* on the whiteboard. Ask what the three phrases have in common. *(The same letters are used in all phrases.)* Discuss how finding anagrams will help students play *Scrabble*. Have students practice finding anagrams on paper before playing *Scrabble*.

> In a whole-group instructional setting with older students, set up a *Scrabble* tournament. Work with your students to create a tournament bracket, matching students against each other until there are only two students left in the tournament. At this point, connect your mobile device to a projector. Display the final *Scrabble* match for the class to watch.

At Home

> Challenge your child to use their school spelling words in a game of *Scrabble*.

> Work with your child to complete a game versus the computer or another family member. Encourage your child to look for several words using his or her seven letters. Explain that it will help him or her find the best word to score the most points.

> Invite your family to play a game in Pass 'N Play mode.

Literary Analysis Guide

Gatsby's Light

Suggested Grades
6–12

Available
iTunes, Google Play

Description

Study the literary elements of prose, poetry, and rhetoric using the interactive graphic wheels. Tap on the literary terms spaced around the analysis wheels to read detailed definitions, examples from literature, and useful questions that solidify your understanding of the term. *Literary Analysis Guide* includes the following key features:

> Graphic wheels to help visualize how style and meaning are developed

> Wheels organized by prose, poetry, and rhetoric

> Over 40 detailed literary entries, including an additional "figure of speech" wheel

At School

> In a whole-group instructional setting, connect your mobile device to a projector. Use the app to supplement your lesson on the literary elements of prose, poetry, and rhetoric.

> Instruct students to write a short story, making sure to incorporate literary elements. Then, place students into pairs and have them read each other's stories. Direct them to write a literary analysis of their partner's story, giving an example of how each literary element was used. Tell them that their analysis should cover at least five elements. Allow them to use the app as a reference guide.

At Home

> Encourage your child to use the app as a reference guide when reading assigned books from school or when writing about books he or she has read.

> Discuss with your child how the literary elements are similar, different, or the same for poetry, prose, and rhetoric.

> After using *Literary Analysis Guide*, challenge your child to find literary elements in movies or television shows. For example, a character in a movie may tell an anecdote that sheds light on his or her personality and past while at the same time moving the plot forward.

Amazing Mathematics Apps

How I Use My Apps

Monkey Math
School Sunshine

THUP Games, LLC

Suggested Grades
Pre-K–1

Available
iTunes

Description

Have fun in the sun with this beach-themed math app. Learn number recognition, comparing numbers, counting, number formation, patterns, shapes, adding and subtracting, and size, while your furry guide monkeys around. Collect prizes to fill your virtual aquarium! *Monkey Math School Sunshine* includes the following key features:

> Nine interactive games

> Intuitive interface to help children discover and choose the correct answers

> Adjusts the level of difficulty for each player

> A monkey guide who celebrates correct answers

At School

> In a whole-group instructional setting, connect your mobile device to a projector. Display *Monkey Math School Sunshine* to demonstrate how to use the game. Ask for volunteers to complete a few rounds of the interactive games in front of the class. Have students that do not volunteer make observations about the game-play and suggest strategies to choose the correct answers.

> Place this app in a center and allow students to build fundamental math skills.

> In pairs, instruct students to take turns playing the interactive math games.

> In teacher-led small groups, have students work with manipulatives to help answer the questions that require addition and subtraction.

At Home

> Work with your child to complete each type interactive math game. Then, have your child work independently while you monitor his or her progress.

> Encourage your child to think about his or her answer carefully before making a selection. Demonstrate the difference between guessing and calculating.

> After using *Monkey Math School Sunshine,* work with your child on the same math concepts using objects in the world around you. For example, have him or her count the number of cereal pieces that are left floating in a bowl of milk, and then count down as the remaining pieces are eaten.

Park Math

Duck Duck Moose, Partnership

Suggested Grades
Pre-K–2

Available
iTunes

Description

Play at the park with Blue Bear and his friends while learning to count, add, subtract, and complete patterns. Enjoy seven educational activities, like counting while feeding the hippo or watching the rabbit swing, putting the dogs in order from small to large, and balancing the mice on a seesaw. *Park Math* includes the following key features:

> Instrumental music that plays popular nursery rhymes with cello and guitar

> Three levels of increasing difficulty

> Engaging activities with colorful art and animations

At School

> Place this app in a center and allow students to play a level that is appropriate for their academic needs—level 1 being the easiest and level 3 being the most difficult.

> In pairs, instruct students to take turns choosing a park activity. Have students take turns completing math activities, helping each other if needed.

> In teacher-led small groups, assist students in creating park activities they would have liked to play in *Park Math*. Help them decide how the activity would work, and have them create a math problem.

> In a whole-group instructional setting, connect your mobile device to a projector. Display *Park Math* and ask for volunteers to complete a few activities in front of the class. Ask for more volunteers to offer strategies for completing activities.

At Home

> Show your child that there are two ways to navigate from one activity to the next. Demonstrate how to swipe Blue Bear forward and backward and how to tap the kites to pick a new activity.

> Have your child work through several of the activities and explain to you how he or she is choosing answers to complete each activity.

> After using *Park Math*, encourage your child to practice math skills at a real-life park. Ask him or her questions such as "How many children would be on the jungle gym if two children went home?"

Paint My Wings

Toca Boca

Suggested Grades
Pre-K–3

Available
iTunes

Description

Fingerpaint the butterfly with perfect symmetry. Begin your masterpiece, and listen to the butterflies teach you the names of colors. Watch as the colors form identical patterns on both sides of the butterfly's wings. Don't forget to tickle the butterflies to hear them laugh! *Paint My Wings* includes the following key features:

> Three different butterflies that say the names of colors as you choose them.

> A variety of paintbrushes

> Save option

At School

> In a whole-group instructional setting, connect your mobile device to a projector. Display a pre-painted symmetrical butterfly made with *Paint My Wings*. Ask students to make observations about the butterfly, such as if they notice anything similar about both sides of the butterfly's wings. Explain the concept of symmetry.

> In teacher-led small groups, have students create a list of objects that are symmetrical. To give them an idea, draw an image of a face on the board and add a dashed line down the center of the face so that each side is symmetrical. Then, draw various shapes that have symmetry and with which students are familiar. Have students help you draw the lines of symmetry for each shape. Explain that each side of the dashed line is a mirror image of the other side.

> Place this app in a center and allow students to paint butterflies with symmetry.

At Home

> Watch as your child paints the butterfly. Ask him or her what color paint is being used. Ask what is happening on the opposite side of the wing as he or she draws. Encourage your child to say the name of a color before it is selected.

> Print your child's symmetrical butterfly from your mobile device's photo album and hang it on the wall for the whole family to enjoy!

> After using *Paint My Wings*, work with your child to spot colors and symmetrical objects in the world around you.

Coin Math

Recession Apps

Suggested Grades
K–3

Available
iTunes

Description

Coin Math is a fun and interactive way to learn how to recognize, count, add, and make change using U.S. coins. Children will also love the shopping simulation that provides money practice through buying items from a store. *Coin Math* includes the following key features:

> Practice with counting by 5s, 10s, and 25s

> Images showing both sides of coins

> Beginning, Intermediate, and Advanced levels

> Audio instructions to help younger learners

At School

> Place this app in a center, and direct students to use the level that best suits their learning needs.

> In pairs, have students take turns using the coins to count money, match coins to their values, or shop.

> In teacher-led small groups, have students work together to match coins. Each student can drag and drop a coin to match with its correct value. Have students count the coins as a group, and choose one student to tap the corresponding value.

> In a whole-group instructional setting, connect your mobile device to a projector. Ask students to name U.S. coins, and record their answers on the whiteboard. Then, display the *What the Coins Look Like* page to introduce new coins and review coins they already know. Have students take turns reading about each coin.

At Home

> Review the U.S. coins with your child, and assist him or her in using the coins to count money, match coins to their values, or shop.

> After using *Coin Math*, create a store in your house. Help your child attach price tags to various household items he or she wants in the store. Take turns being the customer or the shop assistant, allowing your child to practice making change or purchasing items with coins.

Motion Math Zoom

Motion Math

Suggested Grades
K–6

Available
iTunes

Description

It is up to you to put the numbers back where they belong! Zoom in or stretch the number line to drop numbers into the right place. Meet the animals that represent each place value. *Motion Math Zoom* includes the following key features:

> Concrete objects that represent abstract numbers

> Practice with negative numbers, decimals, and basic numbers

> Timed challenge for advanced learners

> Engaging animal animations and sound effects

> Records high scores

At School

> Place this app in a center and allow students to master place value.

> In pairs, instruct students to take turns dropping numbers into their correct places.

> In teacher-led small groups, have students tell you whether to zoom in or out and where to place the numbers. Ask if the number is greater than or less than the previous number.

> In a whole-group instructional setting, connect your mobile device to a projector. Display the number line, and ask students to help you put the numbers where they belong. Ask why the decimal numbers, such as 0.01, have small animals and not big animals representing them.

At Home

> With your child, drop several numbers into their correct place on the number line, and then watch them try it on their own. Choose the number category that is most appropriate for your child's grade level.

> After using *Motion Math Zoom*, work with your child to spot numbers in the world around you. When you spot multiple numbers at a time, have your child place them in order from smallest to largest.

MathBoard

Pala software, Inc.

Suggested Grades
1–8

Available
iTunes

Description

MathBoard offers chalkboard-style math practice. With a wide range of customizable settings to tailor quiz questions, this app will fit your students' academic needs. *MathBoard* includes the following key features:

> Generates random equations with up to 250 questions per quiz

> Equation types such as addition, subtraction, multiplication, division, squared numbers, cubed numbers, and square roots

> Option to time quizzes in elapsed or countdown mode

> Answer styles including multiple choice, fill-in-the-blank, and keypad entry

> Problem Solver that provides steps needed to solve equations

> Option to save quiz results

At School

> Use *MathBoard* to generate quiz and homework questions for students.

> Place this app in a center and have students take a math quiz appropriate for their learning needs.

> Encourage students to use the Problem Solver feature when they answer incorrectly.

> In a whole-group instructional setting, connect your mobile device to a projector. Use *MathBoard*'s Problem Solver feature to demonstrate how to solve specific types of mathematics problems.

At Home

> Set *MathBoard* options to match the math curriculum your child is studying. Set a performance goal with your child. Then, have him or her work to achieve that goal.

> Work with your child to solve quiz questions. Use the Problem Solver feature when necessary.

> Have your child take the same quiz multiple times to improve his or her score and build fluency.

© Shell Education

Splash Math-3rd grade
StudyPad, Inc.

Suggested Grades
2–4

Available
iTunes

Description

Splash Math-3rd grade covers over 200 fundamental math skills with an engaging and fun ocean theme as a backdrop. Every child begins on the Easy level and progresses at his or her own pace, eventually unlocking the Medium and Hard levels. In between solving problems, stop by the aquarium to feed and play with the fun sea creatures. *Splash Math-3rd grade* is also available for grades 1 and 2. *Splash Math-3rd grade* includes the following key features:

> Interactive math problems

> Sixteen math topics, including addition, subtraction, multiplication, division, geometry, decimals, fractions, probability, and money

> Option to email student progress to teacher or parent

At School

> Place this app in a center and allow students to practice math skills.

> In pairs, instruct students to take turns solving math problems.

> In a whole-group instructional setting, connect your mobile device to a projector. Set up a user called "Class." Use this profile for group learning sessions. Enter the app's Play or Practice mode, and have students work as a class to achieve progress within each chapter. Work together to unlock the medium and hard levels. After the class has progressed, award students with a paper aquarium for the classroom wall that mirrors the aquarium in the app. Use blue butcher paper for the water. Then, allow students to cut out, paint, or draw sea creatures to add to the aquarium.

At Home

> Enter the app's practice mode, and have your child pick a chapter he or she would like to play.

> Encourage your child by telling him or her that you are setting up the email reports so you can watch as he or she progresses through all of the 16 chapters. When you see that he or she is progressing, tell him or her how proud you are.

Math Bingo

ABCya.com

Suggested Grades
2–5

Available
iTunes

Description

It is bingo with a math twist! Your goal is to line up five bingo bugs in a row by solving math problems. Get high scores and earn bingo bugs to catapult in the bingo bungee reward game. Choose from five games and three levels of difficulty. *Math Bingo* includes the following key features:

> Addition, Subtraction, Multiplication, Division, and Mixed Practice modes

> Displays correct answer when a wrong answer is selected

> Option to create up to five different player profiles

> Scoreboard that keeps track of scores for each game and level

At School

> Place this app in a center and allow students to select a game and level of difficulty appropriate for their academic needs.

> In pairs, instruct students to take turns solving the math problems. Encourage them to wait until they collect four bingo bugs before playing the bingo bungee game. Explain to students that this will help them get as many coins as possible.

> After using *Math Bingo*, have students make their own math bingo game cards. Using paper and markers, have students create five columns headed with *B, I, N, G*, and *O*. Instruct them to fill in the empty spaces on the bingo card with numbers between 0–20. On index cards, write math problems with answers between 0–20. Draw the cards randomly during the game.

At Home

> Challenge your child to use mental math to solve equations. Provide helpful mental math tips.

> Show your child where the bingo bugs are collected. Encourage your child to collect over 10 bugs so he or she can win all the coins in the bingo bungee game.

> Set up a *Math Bingo* family tournament. After your child has collected over 10 bingo bugs, have each family member play the bingo bungee game to see who can get the highest score.

Everyday Mathematics®
Baseball Multiplication™

McGraw-Hill School Education Group

Suggested Grades
2–5

Available
iTunes

Description

Play a three-inning baseball game as you practice multiplication facts. Once you're up to bat, the pitcher will pitch a multiplication problem. Your correct answer will score a single, a double, a triple, or a home run! *Addition Top-It™, Subtraction Top-It™, and Beat the Computer™ Multiplication* apps are also available by McGraw-Hill. *Everyday Mathematics Baseball Multiplication* includes the following key features:

> Game play with one or two players

> Practice with multiplication facts (1–6)

> Option to play in guided mode

> Game tutorial

At School

> In a whole-group instructional setting, connect your mobile device to a projector. Have students watch the game tutorial, steps one through eight. Then, divide the class into two teams. One team will represent Player 1 and the other will represent Player 2. Begin the *Everyday Mathematics Baseball Multiplication* game. Have students take turns coming up to bat. The team with the most runs wins!

> Place this app in a center and allow students to practice multiplication facts.

> In pairs, have students challenge each other to a game of *Baseball Multiplication*.

At Home

> Watch the game tutorial with your child. Then, challenge your child to a game of *Baseball Multiplication*.

> After using *Everyday Mathematics Baseball Multiplication*, watch a real-life baseball game with your child. Every time a player comes up to bat, challenge him or her to answer a multiplication problem before the player makes it to first base. For every correct answer, your child scores a run. For every answer he or she misses, you score a run. The player with the most runs wins.

Math Wars

Life Skills Games

Suggested Grades
2–6

Available
iTunes

Description

Fly through the galaxy shooting laser beams at numbers in this arcade-style math game. Use the laser cannon crosshairs to locate the answer to your addition, subtraction, multiplication, or division problems, and shoot accurately to get the highest score! *Math Wars* includes the following key features:

> Multiple levels of difficulty

> Practice for math concepts such as addition, subtraction, multiplication, and division

> Fast-action game play

At School

> Place this app in a center and allow students to play a level, selecting a problem type that is appropriate for their academic needs.

> In pairs, allow students to take turns playing *Math Wars*.

> In a whole-group instructional setting, direct students to make their own math-facts flash cards to help sharpen their mental math skills. Encourage them to use the flash cards prior to playing *Math Wars,* since high scores require quick thinking.

> Set up a *Math Wars* tournament. Work with your students to create a tournament bracket, matching students against each other to see who can score the highest. Eliminate players with lower scores, and play until there are only two students remaining in the tournament. At this point, connect your mobile device to a projector. Display the final *Math Wars* match for the class to watch.

At Home

> Set up a *Math Wars* family tournament. Allow your child to choose the level of difficulty and the problem type for the tournament. Or, have family members compete in the addition, subtraction, multiplication, and division levels. Add scores from each round to determine an ultimate winner.

> While spending time with your child driving to and from school, standing in line at the grocery store, or doing chores at home, fill the time by asking your child to solve mental math problems, which will help when playing *Math Wars*.

Rocket Math

Dan Russell-Pinson

Suggested Grades
K–8

Available
iTunes

Description

Build your own rocket and blast into space on a math mission! Tap floating objects, such as stars, coins, clocks, and 3-D shapes that surround your rocket to earn a bronze, silver, or gold medal. Practice your math skills and earn money to build new rocket parts! *Rocket Math* includes the following key features:

> 56 different math missions for practicing numbers/fractions/decimals, counting, telling time, United States money, shapes (2-D and 3-D), patterns, addition, subtraction, multiplication, division, square roots, and more

> Missions ranging in difficulty

> More than 90 rocket parts to build a rocket

> Rocket simulator powered by a realistic physics engine

> Up to five player profiles

At School

> In a whole-group instructional setting, connect your mobile device to a projector. Demonstrate how to build and launch a rocket and earn money for rocket parts.

> Place this app in a center and allow students to practice math skills. Encourage students to choose an appropriate level of difficulty for their math missions.

> In pairs, instruct students to take turns completing math missions, as well as building and launching rockets.

At Home

> Complete a math mission with your child. Then, watch him or her try one on their own. Choose missions that are appropriate for your child's grade level.

> Demonstrate how to earn money by practicing math. Then, show your child the extra rocket parts they can buy.

> Have a math mission contest. See which family member can launch a rocket into space for the longest amount of time. See which family member can earn the gold medal first!

TanZen

Little White Bear Studios, LLC

Suggested Grades
2–8

Available
iTunes

Description

The challenge is on! Sharpen your problem-solving skills by combining all seven geometric pieces into a single shape. Choose one of over 500 entertaining puzzles, and get started. If you are a tangram pro, set the game to the advanced mode. *TanZen* includes the following key features:

> A variety of puzzle difficulty levels

> Keeps track of puzzles in progress

> Easy-to-use touch controls

> Puzzle restart when mobile device is shaken

At School

> In a whole-group instructional setting, connect your mobile device to a projector. Demonstrate how to use the app by showing students how to turn, flip, and move shapes. Research and briefly discuss the history and origin of tangram puzzles with students to increase student engagement and interest.

> Place this app in a center for students to work independently or in pairs. Have students explore the different shapes and sizes of pieces available in the puzzles as well as the different puzzle pictures. Have them explain the object of tangrams in their own words.

> In pairs, instruct students to take turns fitting a shape into the puzzle. Or, have students compete by using a timer to see who can complete the puzzle faster.

At Home

> Demonstrate how to manipulate the tangram shapes. Solve a puzzle with your child before allowing him or her to do one independently.

> After using *TanZen*, encourage your child to build a paper tangram puzzle for a family member to solve. Assist your child in cutting out the tangram shapes, using sturdy paper. Have him or her trace the tangram puzzle's outline on another sheet of paper. Fit the shapes into the outline to complete the tangram.

© Shell Education

FETCH! LUNCH RUSH

PBS Kids

Suggested Grades
1–2

Available
iTunes

Description

The cartoon dog, Ruff Ruffman, is making a movie and needs your help to feed his movie crew. Take sushi orders by completing addition and subtraction problems and then fetch the lunch orders from around your house or classroom. *FETCH! LUNCH RUSH* helps children form a connection between numeric symbols and real life objects. *FETCH! LUNCH RUSH* includes the following key features:

> Increasingly difficult game play that reinforces early algebraic concepts

> Augmented reality (requires mobile devices with built-in cameras)

At School

> Hang the game pieces around the classroom next to objects that represent each number. For example, the game piece with the number 4 can be placed next to four pencils, providing students with an additional visual reference.

> In a whole-group instructional setting, ask for 10 students to act as Number Keepers by holding the printed game pieces. Divide the remaining students into teams. Tell students to complete math problems and then gather a matching number of items to present to the Number Keeper of the same number. The Number Keeper will then allow the student to scan the game piece.

> After completing a lesson on bar graphs, have students play the app to reinforce the concepts learned. Discuss how the stacks of sushi in the game are similar to and different from a bar graph. Direct students to add bars to their bar graph after each math problem by using the corresponding number on the game piece.

At Home

> Work with your child to prepare child-friendly sushi. For example, spread peanut butter over a tortilla, add fruit, roll it up, and slice it into pieces. Have 10 plates of sushi that range from one to 10 pieces per plate. Set the game piece next to the corresponding plate. Play the app with your child, and enjoy the tasty sushi after!

> Hang the game pieces in various locations around your house. Send your child on a scavenger hunt to locate each game piece. Have him or her report back to you before completing the next math problem.

Everyday Mathematics® Equivalent Fractions™

McGraw-Hill School Education Group

Suggested Grades
3–6

Available
iTunes

Description

Earn points as you match equivalent fraction cards. Work with halves, thirds, fourths, fifths, sixths, eighths, tenths, and twelfths. The game is over when all equivalent fractions have been matched, or when there are no more matches to make. *Everyday Mathematics Equivalent Fractions* includes the following key features:

> Fraction practice using visual representations

> Drag and drop fraction cards

> Answer feedback

> Game tutorial

At School

> In a whole-group instructional setting, connect your mobile device to a projector. Have students watch the game tutorial, steps one through seven. Then, have the class work together to match equivalent fractions. Allow students to take turns dragging and dropping the fraction cards as directed.

> Place this app in a center and allow students to match equivalent fractions.

> In pairs, have students challenge each other to an equivalent fraction match. Tell students to each play a round to see who can score the highest number of points.

> In teacher-led small groups, review equivalent fractions with flash cards. Then, play the game as a group.

At Home

> Watch the tutorial with your child, and answer any questions he or she has about equivalent fractions. Then, play the game together.

> For an extra challenge, have your child use a timer while he or she makes matches. Have him or her try to beat the time in a new round.

Motion Math HD

Motion Math

Suggested Grades
3–6

Available
iTunes

Description

Help a fallen star shoot back into space by dropping fractions into the correct places on a number line. Multiple representations of fractions, decimals, and percents are included to help students visualize each part of a whole. The appealing graphics make this app entertaining and fun. *Motion Math HD* includes the following key features:

> Increasing game speeds for extra challenge

> Problem hints

> Beginner, Medium, and Hard modes

> Option to challenge a friend

At School

> Place this app in a center and allow students to practice placing fractions, decimals, and percents on a number line in the app. Select a difficulty level appropriate for each student's academic needs.

> In pairs, instruct students to take turns completing alternating levels. Have them pause the game sporadically to write number statements comparing two of the falling fractions using the terms *less than*, *greater than*, and *equal to*.

> In teacher-led small groups, have students review how fractions, decimals, and percents are related on a number line before playing *Motion Math HD*.

> In a whole-group instructional setting, connect your mobile device to a projector. Set the app's difficulty level to Expert. Then, demonstrate how to play the app. Have students give you directions to place each number in the correct spot on the number line.

At Home

> Show your child how to use the app using the in-game tutorial. Give your child verbal cues, such as "Move it to the right" or "Move it a little to the left."

> Challenge your child to find the correct place for each fraction by the second bounce. For an extra challenge, encourage him or her to find the correct place on the first bounce. Have your child try to beat his or her previous score.

Math Dictionary for Kids

Prufrock Press Inc.

Suggested Grades
3–8

Available
iTunes

Description

Math Dictionary for Kids is a best-selling book turned app. Whether they need to convert Celsius to Fahrenheit or brush up on formulas, kids will keep this handy reference app close during homework sessions. *Math Dictionary for Kids* includes the following key features:

> Over 400 illustrated math terms in categories, including measurement, algebra, geometry, fractions, decimals, statistics, probability, and problem solving

> Option to take notes, mark a subject as a favorite, or explore related terms

> Alphabetical scroll list

> **Lightbulb** button that pulls up a random dictionary entry

> Option to email and print information from the app

At School

> Place this app in a center, and allow students to refer to it while completing math-related assignments.

> In pairs, have students complete a math scavenger hunt. Have them locate several math terms and write one or two facts about each term. The terms they search can correspond to topics currently being covered in the classroom.

> In teacher-led small groups, encourage students to use the reference app to find an answer to a question.

> In a whole-group instructional setting, connect your mobile device to a projector. Use this app to supplement your lesson by displaying definitions or the quick reference tabs.

At Home

> Have your child explain how to use this app. Point out key functions he or she forgot to mention during the app tour.

> Use this app to assist your child with his or her math homework. Encourage your child to look up math terms he or she encounters during homework but doesn't understand. Read the definition with your child, and have him or her summarize it.

Slice It!

Com2uS Inc.

Suggested Grades
3–8

Available
iTunes, Google Play, Amazon

Description

The objective of *Slice It!* is to cut polygons into equal pieces. It is more difficult than you might think! Just how do you slice a square into nine pieces that are equal in size? Accuracy is a *must* if you want to collect all five stars in each brain-teasing level. *Slice It!* includes the following key features:

> Over 200 levels of increasing difficulty

> Slice it Quick timed mode

> Extra obstacles that add to each challenge

> Hints

At School

> In a whole-group instructional setting, connect your mobile device to a projector. As you demonstrate how to use the app, explain to students that they will need to visualize the different shapes that a polygon can be sliced into to make the specified number of equal pieces. Then, facilitate a discussion that will supplement a recent mathematics lesson. For example, you may want to discuss fractions or shapes in relation to this app.

> Place this app in a center and allow students to slice shapes. Encourage them to plan out how they will divide the shape to get equal sizes before they start slicing.

> In pairs, have students play in the Slice it Quick mode to see who can slice the shape with the most accuracy in 60 seconds or less.

At Home

> Work with your child to slice shapes into equal pieces. Discuss strategies and best practices with your child that will help him or her cut the polygons into equal pieces in the required number of slices.

> Encourage your child to play Slice it Quick for an extra challenge. Have him or her try to beat a previous score.

> To strengthen problem-solving skills, help your child discover multiple solutions for each puzzle.

Elevated Math

Elevated Lab Press

Suggested Grades
4–8

Available
iTunes

Description

Make your students' school day more engaging by adding *Elevated Math* to your lesson plan. Choose from over 170 math lessons to use with instruction or intervention. Each interactive lesson includes fun cartoon animations, and cheerful character voices that teach students about math. *Elevated Math* includes the following key features:

> Lessons based on Common Core, NCTM, and state standards for mathematics

> Lessons that cover standards in mathematics categories including Numbers and Operations, Measurement, Geometry, Algebra, and Data Analysis and Probability

> Career-oriented videos demonstrating how math skills are used in the real world

> Three complimentary lessons

> Access to teacher notes and student reproducibles on the *Elevated Math* website

At School

> In a whole-group instructional setting, connect your mobile device to a projector. Inspire kids to learn math by displaying the career video *Jazz Musician*. Provide students with sheet music and have them practice assigning fractions to different note values, such as whole notes ($\frac{1}{1}$), half notes ($\frac{1}{2}$), quarter notes ($\frac{1}{4}$), eighth notes ($\frac{1}{8}$), and sixteenth notes ($\frac{1}{16}$).

> In teacher-led small groups, display the two lessons *Geometry Problems with One Variable* and *Decimals/Fractions/Percent Equivalents* using a projector. During each lesson's practice set, pause the video and have students solve each problem. Then, watch the solution procedures as a class. Facilitate a discussion with students about the best practices to follow for each concept taught.

At Home

> Choose lessons that will supplement the subject matter your child is learning in school. For younger children, complete lessons and activities together. Have older children work independently. Encourage your child to teach you the concepts he or she has learned using the app.

> Watch the career videos with your child to show applied math skills in the real world. Have him or her choose a career to research and learn more about.

Real Kakuro

Deucher

Suggested Grades
3–12

Available
iTunes

Description

Real Kakuro is a fun math version of a crossword puzzle. Each row or column must add up to the number clue given at the beginning of every row and column. *Careful!* You can only use the numbers 1–9 one time in each row or column. *Real Kakuro* includes the following key features:

> Concise, illustrated directions

> Auto-save function

> Choice of puzzles that are Easy, Medium, Hard, Challenging, or Extreme

At School

> Place this app in a center, and direct students to read the instructions on how to play before attempting a puzzle.

> In pairs, have students work together to solve a puzzle.

> In a whole-group instructional setting, connect your mobile device to a projector. Display a Kakuro puzzle that is an appropriate level of difficulty for your class. Explain that Kakuro is a cross between Sudoku and a crossword puzzle. Work through the puzzle as a group, making sure your students understand how to play before attempting one independently or in pairs.

At Home

> Before playing *Real Kakuro*, you may choose to complete a Sudoku and crossword puzzle with your child. Explain that Kakuro is a cross between the two puzzles.

> Work through a Kakuro puzzle with your child. Help him or her devise an effective strategy for completing the puzzles. Have your child write out step-by-step directions, if necessary.

> Practice adding numbers with your child to help him or her increase mental-math accuracy when playing *Real Kakuro*.

Sudoku HD

CrowdCafé

Suggested Grades
4–12

Available
iTunes

Description

Give your brain a workout with *Sudoku HD,* a logic-based number game. Fill in the 9 × 9 grid with numbers so that each row, column, and sub-square uses the numbers 1–9 exactly once. Getting stuck? Tap the auto-fill feature to automatically fill in numbers to help you get ahead. *Sudoku HD* includes the following key features:

› Thousands of puzzles

› Easy, Normal, Hard, and Insane difficulty levels

› Statistics record of fastest puzzle completion times

› Auto-save

› Old Style or Modern themes

At School

› Have older students read the Help screen if they are unfamiliar with the game. Then, allow them to work in pairs or independently.

› In pairs, instruct students to work together. Have them take turns filling in numbers on the grid.

› In a whole-group instructional setting with younger students, connect your mobile device to a projector. Display a Sudoku puzzle that is an appropriate level of difficulty for your class. Explain the object of Sudoku and work through a puzzle as a group. Encourage students to discuss and justify the numbers that they place.

At Home

› Show your child how to use the app. Explain the object of the game, and demonstrate the best ways to begin a puzzle. Ask your child questions, such as whether a sub-square needs a number 8 or whether numbers are missing from a certain row.

› Work through a Sudoku puzzle with your child. Help him or her devise an effective strategy for completing the puzzle. Write out step-by-step directions on how to solve the puzzle, if necessary.

© Shell Education

Amazing Science Apps

How I Use My Apps

Discovery Kids Sharks

Parragon, Inc.

Suggested Grades
K–6

Available
iTunes

Description

Explore the *Discovery Kids Sharks* app, and learn amazing facts, such as where dogfish sharks live, what horn sharks eat, and how big leopard sharks are when they are born. This app includes over 150 shark facts mixed in with fun activities, awesome animations, and heart-stopping footage of sharks in their natural habitats. *Discovery Kids Sharks* includes the following key features:

> Striking photos of sharks

> Facts about shark anatomy, the differences among sharks, how sharks hunt and eat, where they live, and shark families

> Video footage from the Discovery® Channel's *Shark Week*™

> 32 shark trading cards

At School

> Divide the class into groups and have them use the app to explore different types of sharks. Have students choose a shark to learn more about. Instruct students to use the Internet or library to complete their research.

> After using the app, have younger students share with the class an interesting fact they learned about sharks. Ask them what their favorite sharks are and why.

> Have older students write acrostic poems about a type of shark featured in the app. Instruct them to write the name of the type of shark vertically on a piece of paper. Have them write a short phrase starting with each letter, providing facts they learned about that particular type of shark.

At Home

> Help your child collect all 32 shark trading cards by reading each chapter and completing the activities. After all the cards are collected, play a game of "Guess That Shark." To play, read five trading cards with your child. Then read a fact from one of the those five, having your child guess to which shark the fact belongs.

> After using the app, organize a family shark week with your child. Encourage each family member to host a different night of the week. Each host should become an expert of one type of shark and lead a discussion about that type of shark.

Star Walk

Vito Technology, Inc.

Suggested Grades
2–8

Available
iTunes

Description

Point your mobile device at the sky to see the stars, constellations, and planets that are above you. Tap on one of these celestial bodies, and then tap on the **Information** button to learn more. Enter the Sky Live mode to track the moon phases and the rising and setting times of planets, the sun, and the moon. *Star Walk* includes the following key features:

> Searches and locates constellations, planets, nebulas, clusters, galaxies, stars, satellites, and more

> A new featured space picture daily

> Augmented reality (requires mobile devices with built-in cameras)

At School

> Place this app in a center and allow students to explore space. First, choose a planet in our solar system. Have students locate the planet in the app and tap the **Information** button to learn more about the planet. Then, have students create a scavenger hunt using the app. Instruct them to write clues to help others locate and record the coordinates of one satellite, two planets, three stars, and a galaxy.

> In pairs, instruct students to use the app to draw a star map of a small portion of space. Have them include at least one constellation in their maps. Tell them to label and record the coordinates for each major star in the constellations they chose.

> Using the Sky Live mode in the menu, track the phases of the moon over the last month. Have students fill in blank calendar days with a sketch of the moon phase, its name, the time the moon rose and set, and the date.

At Home

> Help your child use the app to locate constellations in the sky. Ask what each constellation's shape represents. Help your child search the Internet or books at the library to discover how different constellations got their names.

> Show your child the Time Machine mode in the top-right corner of the screen. Tap the icon to see what the view will look like two days from now. Then, see what the stars looked like two years ago. Discuss why the sky is different at these two times.

© Shell Education

Bobo Explores Light

Game Collage, LLC

Suggested Grades
3–8

Available
iTunes

Description

Bobo the robot is ready to take you on an entertaining science adventure in this interactive iBook. Learn about light through hands-on experimentation, videos, articles, animations, and trivia. Initiate Bobo's 3-D holograms with a tap of the finger, or explore the engaging pull-down curtains. *Bobo Explores Light* includes the following key features:

> Brightly colored graphics to engage learners of all ages

> 21 light-related topics, edited by a team of experienced educators

> Over 100 pages of content

> Bobo, a playful guide who whistles, giggles, and dances his way through light exploration

At School

> Place this app in a center and allow students to read independently or in pairs. Have students write at least three new science facts that they learned.

> In pairs, have students choose a topic from *Bobo Explores Light*, such as reflection or refraction, to study further. Allow time for students to research the subject on the Internet or in the school library. Have students present their findings to the class.

> In a whole-group instructional setting, connect your mobile device to a projector. Use one of the 21 light-related topics as an introduction to a lesson on light.

At Home

> Allow your child to choose a topic from the table of contents that they want to explore first. Have them read each page and pull-down curtain before they choose another topic.

> Help your child develop comprehension skills by asking him or her questions about the passage they are reading. Encourage your child to make connections between the science concepts presented and the world around them.

> Encourage your child to discuss what he or she has learned from this app with family and friends.

Discover Your Body HD

Clear Vision Sp. z o.o.

Suggested Grades
3–5

Available
iTunes

Description

Explore different parts of the human body, such as the skeleton, the circulatory system, the pulmonary system, and the nervous system. The interactive activities and humorous sound effects make learning about the human body entertaining and fun. *Discover Your Body HD* includes the following key features:

> Option to display a boy or girl body

> Information about specific parts of the body, such as the skeleton and major internal systems

> Audio playback

At School

> Place this app in a center and have students learn about the different systems of the human body. Have them explore the various features in the app and then assemble the parts of the body.

> In pairs, have students complete the Color the Body activity. Have them take turns identifying different parts of the body. Challenge them to complete the activity a second time, attempting to beat their previous time. Also, have them complete the Assemble the Body activity.

> Divide the class into nine groups. Assign to each group one of the body systems categories presented in the app (found in the Explore the Body section). Using the app, have each group read about the different parts of their assigned system. Have each group draw a diagram of its system and present it to the class.

At Home

> Read the descriptions of each body part with your child. Ask your child *Who, What, When, Where,* and *Why* questions to build his or her comprehension. For example, ask "What do you think would happen to our bodies if our skeletons disappeared?"

> Assemble the body with your child, taking turns putting body parts into place. Or, take turns assembling the entire body in a race to assemble the body. Allow your child to go second so he or she can see where all the parts go while you are assembling.

    © Shell Education

SimplePhysics

Andrew Garrison

Suggested Grades
3–12

Available
iTunes, Google Play, Amazon

Description

Use blueprints to design complex structures, such as tree houses and Ferris wheels that will not break under pressure. Take the certification test to determine if your structure passes or fails various stress tests. Use the finger test to push and pull on your design, or to knock it into pieces! *SimplePhysics* includes the following key features:

> Slow Motion mode for determining how to fix a failing design

> Highlighted beams that show structural design weaknesses

> Realistic physics engine

> Option to email blueprints to friends

> **Undo** button and **Beam Eraser** tool

At School

> Place this app in a center and allow students to work together to design blueprints.

> In pairs, challenge students to see who can make the least expensive structure that also passes the certification test.

> In teacher-led small groups, offer students assistance with the more challenging levels.

> In a whole-group instructional setting, connect your mobile device to a projector. Teach students the geometry skills needed to understand how to build a strong, supported structure. Use the app to supplement your lesson.

At Home

> Work with your child to design a blueprint. Have your child test several designs for the same level in order to lower the cost of his or her structure while also passing the certification test.

> Assist your child in determining the areas in his or her structure that need to be strengthened.

> Encourage your child to research how professionals design buildings in real life and what steps they take to ensure their structures are sturdy and safe.

Science Glossary

Visionlearning, Inc.

Suggested Grades
3–12

Available
iTunes

Description

Science Glossary is a comprehensive collection of scientific terms, figures, and short biographies. This app is sure to be an excellent addition to your learning toolbox. *Science Glossary* includes the following key features:

> Definitions that include links to related glossary entries and learning modules on the Visionlearning website.

> Alphabetized scroll list

> Searchable list

At School

> Place this app in a center and allow students to refer to it while completing science-related assignments.

> In pairs, have students complete a science scavenger hunt. Have them locate several science terms and write one or two facts about each term. The terms they search can correspond to topics currently being covered in the classroom.

> Encourage students to use this app while they work on science classwork. Have them look up answers to their questions before they ask you for the answer.

> In a whole-group instructional setting, connect your mobile device to a projector. Supplement your lesson by displaying glossary definitions while you teach.

At Home

> Have your child choose a topic to read about. Read the passage together, and ask your child questions about the passage to make sure he or she understands the key concepts.

> Keep this app close while watching television. Random science facts pop up from time to time while enjoying your favorite shows. Turn it into a teachable moment and look up the random science topic with your child. Discuss whether the show got the science right or whether they exaggerated to make the story more exciting.

> Encourage your child to look up any unknown science terms that appear in his or her homework. Have your child verbally define the terms they discover.

#50847—110 Amazing Apps for Education
© Shell Education

A Life Cycle App

Nth Fusion LLC

Suggested Grades
4–8

Available
iTunes

Description

Cycles are all around us, which is why it is important for children to understand them. *A Life Cycle App* not only details the life cycles of frogs, butterflies, and plants, but also includes other natural cycles such as the water cycle, moon phases, the nitrogen cycle, and the rock cycle. *A Life Cycle App* includes the following key features:

> Colorfully illustrated cycles

> Child-friendly descriptions for each stage of the cycles

> Audio playback for stage descriptions

At School

> In pairs, allow students to explore the *A Life Cycle App*. Have students write at least five multiple-choice quiz questions for each other. Allow students to grade each other's quizzes.

> Have students write short stories with one of the cycles as a main theme. For example, if the student chooses to write about the life cycle of a frog, he or she could make the tadpole the main character of the story.

> In a whole-group instructional setting with younger students, connect your mobile device to a projector. Display a cycle that will supplement concepts you are currently teaching in the classroom or that will help review concepts already taught. Distribute construction paper to students and have them illustrate the cycle they are learning about. Have them label the cycle and summarize each part.

At Home

> Read the different stages in a cycle with your child. Allow him or her to quiz you about each stage of the cycle.

> Challenge your child to act out the various stages of a cycle. Have family members participate, allowing your child to give them roles and direction in the skit.

> Have your child write an acrostic poem using the title of a cycle he or she chooses. For example, if the cycle is the life cycle of the frog, your child may write the word *FROG* vertically on a piece of paper. Starting with the *F*, he or she will write a word or phrase that helps describe the frog's life cycle.

Puzzle Planets

National Geographic Society

Suggested Grades
4–8

Available
iTunes

Description

Race against the clock while assembling a planet's tectonic plates. Then, smash the plates together to form mountains, and rip them apart to make mid-ocean ridges and volcanic islands. Populate the planet with life before mega natural disasters try to destroy it. *Puzzle Planets* includes the following key features:

> Stunning 3-D graphics

> 15 different planets to create

> 45 alien life forms to collect

At School

> Place this app in a center and have students strengthen their understanding of geologic concepts by assembling the tectonic plates, building mountains and volcanoes, and pulling plates apart to form ridges.

> After using *Puzzle Planets* in a classroom of older students, have students draw humorous cartoons to explain what happens when tectonic plates collide or diverge. Then, instruct students to research which plate boundaries are closest to them. Ask them to research and record some of the data that scientists have collected related to the closest tectonic plate boundary.

> In a whole-group instructional setting with younger students, connect your mobile device to a projector. Use the app as an introduction to plate tectonics. Discuss plate tectonics, convergent plate boundaries, and divergent plate boundaries.

At Home

> Challenge your child to a *Puzzle Planet* competition. See who can create planets the fastest and earn the greatest number of stars.

> Work with your child on strengthening his or her understanding of geological concepts. Search the Internet for a map of Earth that shows the plate boundaries. Point out the different plates. Help your child identify the plate you live on.

> Watch *Clash of the Continents*™ on the National Geographic Channel® to help your child understand the science behind the *Puzzle Planets* app.

Aero!

GameDesk

Suggested Grades
4–12

Available
iTunes

Description

Aero! teaches the basics of aerodynamics in this interactive flight simulator. Use the thumb-sliders to control the albatross as it soars over the ocean, ascending and descending according to the angle of its wings. *Aero!* includes the following key features:

› Realistic flight simulation

› Diagrams explaining the basic concepts of aerodynamics

› Realistic physics engine

At School

› Place this app in a center for students to learn the basics of aerodynamics. Encourage students to read about the dynamics of flight and study the diagrams by tapping the **Question Mark** and **Exclamation Point** buttons.

› In pairs, have older students take turns flying the albatross, testing its flight with its wings at different angles. Then, have them research and compare a bird in flight with an airplane in flight. Ask them to discover the differences.

› In a whole-group instructional setting, connect your mobile device to a projector. Use *Aero!* as an introduction to a lesson on aerodynamics. Use the diagrams as supplements. Discuss the dynamics of flight, including the laws of motion, airflow, lift, and drag.

At Home

› Ask your child if he or she has ever noticed the way birds fly. Facilitate a discussion about your child's observations. Then, have him or her use *Aero!* to explore a bird in flight.

› Review the diagrams together. Have your child explain what he or she understands from the diagrams, and correct any misconceptions.

March of the Dinosaurs

Touch Press LLP

Suggested Grades
4–12

Available
iTunes

Description

Follow the story of Scar and Patch, two young dinosaurs who struggle to survive the harsh Arctic climate and extreme dangers, such as volcanic eruptions, blizzards, and deadly predators. Read over 65 illustrated pages, and meet 10 dinosaurs through the realistic 3-D animations. *March of the Dinosaurs* includes the following key features:

> 12 chapters with over 65 beautifully illustrated pages and digital video clips

> Story narration synchronized with highlighted text

> Fact files about dinosaurs and research notes

> Links to WolframAlpha knowledge engine

At School

> In a whole-group instructional setting with older students, lead a discussion about the *March of the Dinosaurs.* Have students predict how the story's authors knew particular facts about the dinosaurs.

> In a whole-group instructional setting with younger students, connect your mobile device to a projector. Allow students to follow along as the narrator reads *March of the Dinosaurs*. Have them listen to the story in one or multiple sessions.

> In pairs of younger students, have students listen to the story. Allow them to explore the 3-D animated dinosaurs and read the facts about each one. Encourage students to explore the fact files. Then, have them sketch and write a summary about their favorite dinosaur.

> Place this app in a workstation for older students and allow them to read the interactive story and explore the additional features.

At Home

> Read or listen to the interactive storybook with your child. Ask him or her *Who, What, When, Where,* and *Why* questions to build comprehension skills.

> If available, watch the TV special "Escape of the Dinosaurs," produced in partnership with the National Geographic Channel's and BBC's *Walking with Dinosaurs* series.

NASA Visualization Explorer

NASA

Suggested Grades
4–12

Available
iTunes

Description

NASA Visualization Explorer is the coolest way to connect with the latest cutting edge space-based research. New articles, including stunning images and videos, are released on a weekly basis. With its easy-to-use interface, this is the perfect app for space enthusiasts. *NASA Visualization Explorer* includes the following key features:

> Extraordinary satellite images with every article

> Topics, such as climate change, glaciers, hurricanes, volcanoes, and wildfires

> Stories about advanced space-based research

> Cutting-edge research stories presented in an engaging and exciting format

> New stories every week

At School

> Place this app in a center and allow students to read the available articles independently or in pairs. Have students write down at least three new science facts.

> In pairs, have students choose a topic from one of the articles for further study. Allow time to research the subject on the Internet or in the school library. Have students present their topics and findings to the class.

> In a whole-group instructional setting, connect your mobile device to a projector. Use one of the articles as a supplement to a lesson on space or Earth.

At Home

> Allow your child to choose an article on a topic that he or she wants to explore first. Examine the images and help your child read the article together.

> Ask your child about the passage he or she is reading to help develop comprehension skills. Have a discussion with your child to help them internalize an understanding of the topic.

> Encourage your child to discuss what he or she has learned from *NASA Visualization Explorer* with family and friends.

Smash Your Food HD

Food N' Me

Suggested Grades
3–8

Available
iTunes

Description

There's perhaps no better way to learn about nutrition than to crush, explode, pound, and smash unhealthy food to bits. Think you're nutrition savvy? First guess the amount of salt, fat, and oil in each food. Then smash it to see if you were right. *Smash Your Food* includes the following key features:

> Video clips of a smashing machine pulverizing food

> 4 levels of food for free, including a cola drink, French fries, a jelly doughnut, and a cup of noodles

> Bonus level with a Crazy Food item (must provide an email address to access)

> Unlock upwards of 40 foods with the full in-app purchase

At School

> In a whole-group instructional setting, connect your mobile device to a projector. Divide students into teams of four. Play each level as a class, having teams guess the amount of salt, fat, and oil in each food item. Have students write their guesses on a sheet of paper. Then smash the food! Award points to teams based on the closest guesses. Discuss the information in this app as an extension to your science and health curriculum.

> Have students draw additional *Smash Your Food* scenes with included nutritional values listed on the backs of the drawings. Have students share their food drawings and nutrition facts with their peers.

At Home

> Challenge your child to a Smash Your Food 1 on 1 tournament. Write your nutritional guesses on a sheet of paper. Compare your guesses with your child's. Then using the app, smash the food! Award points based on the closest guesses.

> Create an at-home level with your child. Research an unhealthy food and record its nutritional value. Prepare that food at home. Work with your child to create a safe, at-home version of a smashing machine. Then allow your child to guess the nutritional facts for the food item you prepared. Use the smashing machine to crush the food. Compare your child's guesses with the actual nutritional values.

Inside Nature's Giants

Harper Collins Publishers, Ltd

Suggested Grades
4–12

Available
iTunes

Description

Inside Nature's Giants travels the world to explore the anatomy of some of the largest creatures that exist on Earth—by dissecting them! This app includes detailed accounts of their journeys with behind-the-scenes footage, stunning images, and maps to see the animals' habitats. *Inside Nature's Giants* includes the following key features:

> Articles, images, and videos of each animal

> Rotating 3-D animals

> 12 animal adventures with facts about animal anatomy

At School

> Place this app in a center and allow students to read about Earth's giant animals inside and out.

> Divide the class into 12 groups, and assign each group one of the animals in this app. Have students read the articles and take notes about their assigned animal. Then, have each group create a model of its animal using common classroom art supplies. Have groups include descriptions with their models. Then, have the models displayed around the classroom.

> Use butcher paper to make scaled-to-size outlines of the animals featured in this app. In pairs, have students make scaled-to-size outlines of the animal's organs. Pin the animal outline to the wall and attach the organs.

At Home

> Have younger children read an article a day to you. At the end of the 12 days, have your child make a poster displaying information about the animal he or she found most interesting. Help your child take screenshots of images in the app and print them to add to his or her poster.

> Have your child research a giant animal not featured in *Inside Nature's Giants*. Then, encourage your child to write a fictional story about the adventure he or she had finding this animal in the wild and what was learned from dissecting it. Encourage him or her to write a letter to the *Inside Nature's Giants* team to ask a question or to share the story.

VideoScience

Object Enterprises

Suggested Grades
4–12

Available
iTunes

Description

Find the perfect experiment to complete at home or in the classroom. Each lesson comes with a how-to video and step-by-step instructions. With experiments like Neon Waterfall and Alien Egg, children are certain to be inspired! *VideoScience* includes the following key features:

> Over 80 hands-on science lessons

> New experiments added regularly

> Variety of science topics

At School

> Place this app in a center and allow students to watch the science videos independently or in pairs. Have students write at least three science facts they learned.

> In pairs, have students choose a topic from one of the videos for further study. Allow time to research the subject on the Internet or in the school library. Have students present their findings to the class.

> In a whole-group instructional setting, connect your mobile device to a projector. Use one of the videos as a supplement to a science lesson or to get students excited about an upcoming unit.

> Have students watch the science videos to help them develop ideas and questions they will explore to develop science fair projects. Instruct students to write out lists of supplies they will need and the procedures they will follow to carry out their experiments.

At Home

> Allow your child to choose a video that he or she wants to watch. Ask your child why they chose that particular video and discuss the science behind it.

> Work with your child to organize a science show for your family to participate in. Have each family member choose an experiment from the *VideoScience* collection to complete. Allow each family member time to prepare materials and practice their experiment. Then, invite friends over to watch the experiments performed.

Frog Dissection

Emantras Inc

Suggested Grades
6–12

Available
iTunes

Description

Dissect a frog minus the mess! *Frog Dissection* includes all the tools and trappings used in a real classroom dissection. It's the perfect app for students learning about organs and organ systems. After the lifelike procedure is complete, students can tap on the exposed organs to learn more. *Frog Dissection* includes the following key features:

> Step-by-step procedure instructions with voice-over

> Wet lab process instructions

> Human and frog anatomy experience

> Frog life cycle animation

> An interactive quiz, activities, and videos

At School

> Place this app in a center and allow students to build their knowledge about a frog's classification, eating and living habits, special senses, life cycle, digestive system, organs, and ecosystem, as well as to see a comparison of frogs and toads.

> Encourage students to study the wet-lab process instructions before an actual in-class dissection. Follow up by allowing them to use the app after the real procedure to refresh key concepts, procedure steps, and knowledge about organs and organ systems.

> In a whole-group instructional setting, connect your mobile device to a projector. Display the Human Vs Frog comparison chart, and discuss it as a class.

At Home

> Encourage your child to watch the videos and read about frogs before continuing to the virtual dissection activity.

> Have your child illustrate a dissected frog and its organs. Then, have him or her label the organs.

> After your child has completed the virtual dissection, have a discussion with him or her about the importance of dissection.

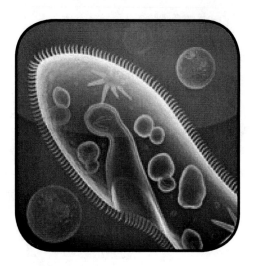

Cell and Cell Structure

Emantras Inc

Suggested Grades
6–12

Available
iTunes

Description

Life's smallest unit is under the microscope, ready for you to take a look! Learn about cells and cell structures through interactive activities and HD quality videos. Then test your knowledge by completing the fun picture quizzes, word searches, and flash cards. *Cell and Cell Structure* includes the following key features:

> High-quality cell diagrams

> Easy-to-navigate interface

> Interactive activities, including word search, flash cards, and a quiz

> Videos of plant and animal cells, including the phases of mitosis for both

At School

> Place this app in a workstation and allow students to explore the app. Instruct them to watch the videos *Inside an Animal Cell* and *Inside a Plant Cell*. Have students write to compare the two types of cells and draw labeled diagrams of both.

> In pairs, have students review the flash cards together. Then, have students quiz each other on the terms presented.

> In whole-group instructional settings, review key concepts students learned about cells and cell structures. Then, allow students time to construct models of plant and animal cells using common objects. Provide students with materials, such as yarn, modeling clay, straws, string, toothpicks, beads, and pipe cleaners.

At Home

> Watch your child take the quiz and check his or her comprehension. Take note of the questions he or she answers incorrectly, so you can review the material and explain any misconceptions.

> Bake or purchase cookies to make cell diagrams. Encourage your child to make a diagram of an animal and plant cell using the cookies with raisins, nuts, and other edibles. Have your child present the plant and animal cell cookies to your family and allow him or her to share knowledge of cells and cell structure.

SkySafari 3 Pro
Southern Stars

Suggested Grades
6–12

Available
iTunes, Google Play

Description

The universe is at your fingertips with this comprehensive astronomy app. It includes a database of over 15 million stars, 740,000 galaxies, and an additional 550,000 objects in space. Explore information about satellites, comets, asteroids, and other celestial bodies. Take this app outside while using the **Night** button to maintain darkness, and point your mobile device toward the sky to learn about the celestial objects that are right above you! *SkySafari 3 Pro* includes the following key features:

> Views of the sky a million years into the past or future

> 1,100 encyclopedic descriptions of celestial bodies

> Over 800 images from NASA

> Sky chart that follows the motion of your mobile device

At School

> Place this app in a center and allow students to explore space. Have students write two facts about five different celestial objects they find while exploring.

> In teacher-led small groups, discuss the terms *magnitude* and *light years*. Have students use *SkySafari 3 Pro* to draw a star map of a section of the sky. Have them label at least three of the stars and include the name, coordinates, and magnitude of each one, as well as the distance each one is from Earth.

> In a whole-group instructional setting, connect your mobile device to a projector. Tap the **SkyWeek** button on the bottom right of the screen to access a list of interactive sky charts. Select the sky chart for the current day of the week, and have students identify what, if any, major sky events are taking place. Check for major sky events in the sky charts for other days of the week.

At Home

> At night, work with your child to locate constellations and stars in the sky using the app to help. Make sure you set the app to Night mode.

> Compare the current placement of the stars above you with a view of that region one month ago, one year ago, 10 years ago, and 100 years ago. Ask your child if each view looks the same or different and why.

Oresome Elements

Intunity Pty Ltd.

Suggested Grades
6–12

Available
iTunes

Description

Race against the clock while dragging and dropping elements into their correct places on the periodic table. Make matches as quickly as possible to score a record time on the Leader Board. Double-tap anywhere on the periodic table to view an element's properties. *Oresome Elements* includes the following key features:

> Includes 109 elements

> An increasing number of elements to pair together over three game levels

> Leader Board that keeps track of record times and progress

> Additional information about each element

At School

> Place this app in a center and allow students to use it to memorize the placement and symbols of elements on the periodic table.

> In pairs, have students compete to see who can beat each level the fastest. Have students add up the time they took for all three levels to determine an ultimate winner.

> Using the app's periodic table, make a list of clues of how particular elements are used. For example, a clue for helium could be "This element is used to make balloons float." Display the clues on the whiteboard, and instruct students to use the clues to discover the elements they describe. Have them first locate the picture of how the element is used, and then have them write down the element's name.

> In a whole-group instructional setting, connect your mobile device to a projector. Use this app as a supplement to a lesson about the periodic table.

At Home

> Work with your child to learn the elements and their corresponding symbols. Help them match each of the symbols to its corresponding element.

> Have your child double-tap on each element. Discuss the listed example. Help your child think of other possible examples of each element. Encourage your child to conduct research, if necessary.

The Elements: A Visual Exploration

Element Collection, Inc

Suggested Grades
6–12

Available
iTunes

Description

This app is much more than a periodic table. It sports smoothly rotating samples of the elements. And with a simple tap, you are taken to a nearly full-screen view of a crystal-clear rotating photograph, along with the element's basic facts. Tap the second page to learn about where the element is found and how it is used. *The Elements: A Visual Exploration* includes the following key features:

> Table of contents and search field

> *The Elements*, an entertaining and animated song by Tom Lehrer

> Over 500 objects to view in 3-D. (3-D glasses sold separately.)

> Embedded WolframAlpha computational knowledge engine

At School

> Place this app in a center and allow students to refer to it while completing chemistry or other science-related assignments.

> Have students select an element that is named after a scientist. Instruct them to research the scientist and element on the Internet or at the school library. Then, have them share their findings with the class.

> In pairs, have students complete an elements scavenger hunt. Have them use the app to collect five facts about 10 different elements.

> In whole-group instructional settings, connect your mobile device to a projector. Begin a lesson on the periodic table by playing *The Elements* song accessed from the Home screen.

At Home

> Watch the video for Tom Lehrer's song *The Elements*. Find the lyrics on the Internet and challenge your child to memorize them. Make it a game and have family members vote on who can perform the song with the most accuracy.

> Ask your child how he or she thinks each element is different. Have your child look for answers to this question by reading the fact pages for each of the elements and by conducting additional research.

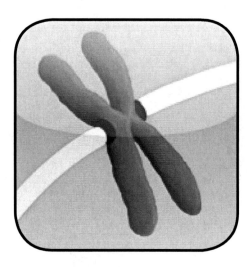

Mitosis

Inkling Systems, Inc.

Suggested Grades
6–12

Available
iTunes

Description

Mitosis is an interactive exploration of cell division. The organized app makes learning painless. Just choose from the simple menu to view videos, images, and links to additional resources. Or, read about the phases of mitosis, and drag and drop parts of a cell to activate an animation displaying that phase. *Mitosis* includes the following key features:

> Images of cells from light microscopes

> Step-by-step visuals and descriptions of the phases of mitosis

> 10-question quiz that gives the correct answer after an incorrect answer is selected

> Links to Wikipedia® articles, YouTube® videos, images from the Botanical Society of America®, articles at NOVA® online, and images from Florida State University

At School

> Place this app in a center and allow students to learn the phases of cell division. Instruct them to watch the videos *Mitosis*, *Through a Microscope*, *The Cell Cycle*, and *Stages of Mitosis*. Have them write a summary of each phase of mitosis in their own words after watching the videos.

> While students read, direct them to pick a topic for further research on the Internet or at the school library.

> In a whole-group instructional setting, review key concepts students learned about cell division. Then, allow students time to construct 3-D models of each phase of mitosis. Provide objects, such as yarn, modeling clay, straws, string, toothpicks, beads, and pipe cleaners.

At Home

> Encourage your child to read about mitosis, watch videos, and take the interactive quiz. Discuss each phase with your child and have him or her describe each one.

> Watch your child take the quiz to check for comprehension. Take note of the questions he or she answers incorrectly so you can review the material and explain any misconceptions.

                        © Shell Education

Amazing Social Studies Apps

How I Use My Apps

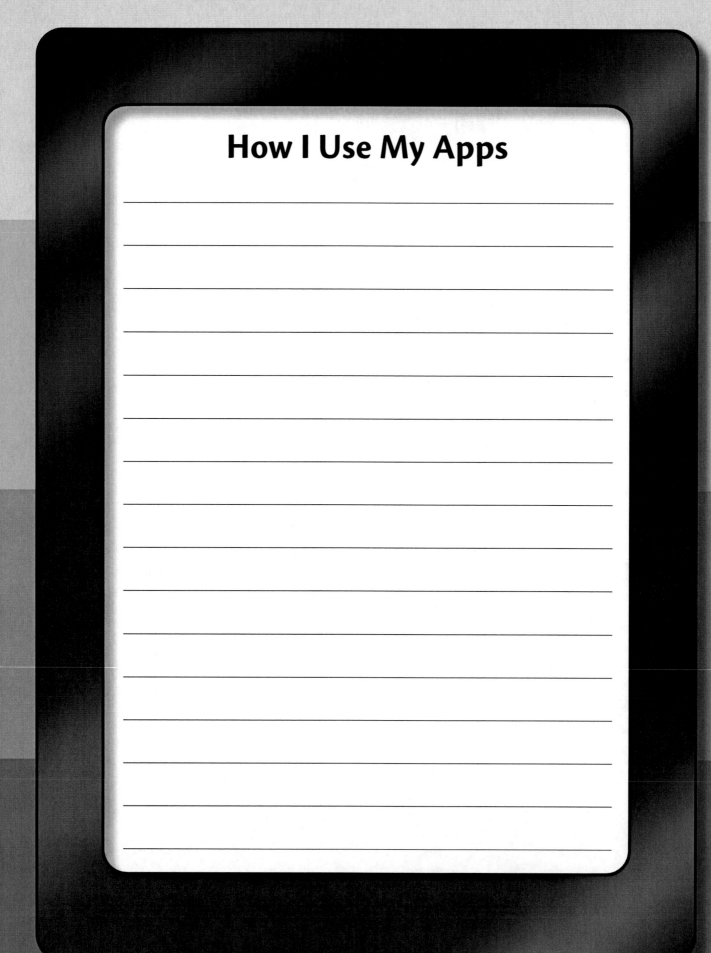

Roxie's a-MAZE-ing Vacation Adventure

OCG Studios

Suggested Grades
Pre-K–3

Available
iTunes

Description

Travel with Roxie in her car, on her skis, and in her raft across 16 screens of adventure. On your interactive expedition around the city, search for letters, numbers, and dozens of objects. Park in the lot and walk through zoos, amusement parks, and more. *Roxie's a-MAZE-ing Vacation Adventure* includes the following key features:

> Multiple player profiles

> A tutorial session for each new player

> Easy-to-use and intuitive interface

At School

> In teacher-led small groups, have a student choose a landmark on the map. Then, have the other students give cardinal directions to navigate Roxie to the landmark.

> In a whole-group instructional setting, connect your mobile device to a projector. Display the first map that Roxie must explore. Ask students what types of places they would see in a community. Then, point out parks, streets, shops, and buildings on the map. Lead a discussion about the important parts of a community.

> In pairs, have students design and draw their own city collage, including streets, parking lots, shops, buildings, and attractions. Instruct them to include letters, numbers, and other objects in their design. Then, have them draw roads that end diagonally in each corner of their maps. Connect students' maps corner to corner to form one giant collage. Hang the collage on an accessible bulletin board. Instruct students to make a map legend that includes all the items for which they can search. Invite other classes to come and enjoy the adventure!

At Home

> Search for objects, letters, and numbers with your child. Have your child give you cardinal directions to lead you to various items you have found together.

> After using *Roxie's a-MAZE-ing Vacation Adventure*, set off on your own vacation adventure. Plot the adventure ahead of time with the help of your child. Draw landmarks onto a real paper map of the city. Give yourselves a time limit to locate every landmark. Then, go and explore the attractions on your map.

The Oregon Trail®

GameLoft S.A.

Suggested Grades
K–12

Available
iTunes, Google Play, Amazon

Description

The Wild West awaits! Climb aboard your wagon to begin a pioneering adventure. Select your wagon companions and departure date, and buy supplies. During your journey, encounter famous historical figures, pass through real places, and acquaint yourself with 19th century pioneer life through historical references. *The Oregon Trail* includes the following key features:

› Eight mini-games, including hunting, fishing, river crossing, wagon repairing, sending messages by telegraph, berry picking, and gold panning

› Character events, such as contracting diseases and encountering bandits and hitchhikers

› Historical sites and figures integrated into every journey

At School

› Place this app in a center and allow students to learn about 19th century pioneer life. Instruct students to choose an appropriate level of difficulty.

› Have students help plan a play based on *The Oregon Trail* game. Have them choose wagon characters and the historical figures the characters meet along the way, and then write a script including these characters. Have students make props and stage sets. Then, invite other classes to watch students perform the play.

› Have students conduct research about the famous historical figures that appear in the game. Have them choose one historical person from the game. Direct students to write a list of questions they would ask this person about 19th century pioneer life. Then, have each student write a biography of that figure.

At Home

› Facilitate a discussion about the Oregon Trail with your child. Explain that the trail spans 2,000 miles from the Missouri River to the valleys in Oregon. Tell your child that people first traveled this trail over a hundred years ago, and it was a long journey. Then, play the game together.

› Have your child help you research the Oregon Trail and consider the accuracy of *The Oregon Trail* game.

Earth Flags HD

OrdWiz.com

Suggested Grades
K–12

Available
iTunes

Description

The flags of the world are at your fingertips with this Google Maps powered app. Listen to a country's anthem as you research the capital city, population, Internet TLD, calling code, and currency. Over 200 foreign lands are included! *Earth Flags HD* includes the following key features:

> Countries organized by continent, by population, and in alphabetical order

> Statistics given for every country, such as flag, capital, total area, and language

> Standard, Satellite, and Hybrid maps

At School

> Have younger students design a class flag. Discuss why flags are important and how they can create a sense of pride, unite people, and be a symbol of ownership. Explain that the class flag should represent all of these things. Instruct them to use colors and shapes that represent the group.

> Have students discuss similarities and differences of flags from around the world. Ask them if they see a common theme among flags. Have students form groups and discuss why countries, provinces, and states have flags; what the flags represent; and why are they important.

> In pairs, have students test each other on how many flags they recognize from around the world. Tell them to first pick a flag, cover up the name, and then ask their partner to name the flag.

At Home

> With your child, make a list of the places and events that display flags from around the world (e.g., *Olympic Games, Embassies, United Nations*).

> Have your child use the app to select two or three flags from around the world that he or she wants to know more about. Allow your child to use the Internet or library to conduct research. Work with your child to figure out why countries choose the colors, emblems, and shapes that are used in their flags.

> Make a family flag with your child. Have him or her choose colors, emblems, and shapes that would best represent your family.

Beautiful Planet HD

Banzai Labs Inc.

Suggested Grades
K–12

Available
iTunes

Description

Beautiful Planet HD features over 580 stunning images taken on seven continents and 160 countries. Travel photographer Peter Guttman has captured the essence of life in his three decades of exploration. *Beautiful Planet HD* includes the following key features:

> Insightful descriptions of each photograph

> Zoomable map

> Option to share pictures on Facebook

> Music player

At School

> In small groups, allow students to explore photos taken at different locations. Then, have them choose one location and create a travel brochure for that location. Explain to students that they should use the photos of their location as a guide to write about the important and interesting aspects of the location they chose.

> In a whole-group instructional setting with older students, connect your mobile device to a projector. Display a picture from the app, and instruct students to write a description of it. Encourage students to make inferences about what might be happening outside the borders of the photograph while writing their descriptions.

> Place this app in a center and allow students to choose one photograph to write a behind-the-scenes article about.

At Home

> Have your child explain to you what is happening in one of the photographs. Ask questions to encourage him or her to give specific details about what is happening in the photo, what might have happened before and after the photo was taken, and what details in the picture could help someone decide where the photo was taken.

> Encourage your child to use one of the photographs as the premise for a story. Ask him or her to tell you about the main characters, what they are trying to accomplish, and what happens along the way. Have your child figure out how the environment affects the characters on their journey.

© Shell Education

Let's create! Pottery

Infinite Dreams

Suggested Grades
K–12

Available
iTunes, Google Play, Amazon

Description

Shape, fire, and paint pottery that you create on a virtual pottery wheel. Add ancient cultural designs, using specialized paintbrushes. Unleash your artistic creativity with this fun and interactive app. *Let's create! Pottery* includes the following key features:

> Realistic pottery wheel

> A variety of paintbrushes featuring Greek, Chinese, Japanese, Egyptian, Aztec, African, Celtic, American Indian, and Neanderthal art

> Coins you can earn to purchase virtual materials, ornaments, paint, and brushes

> Relaxing background sound effects

At School

> In a whole-group instructional setting, connect your mobile device to a projector. Display the app and demonstrate how to use the virtual pottery wheel. Before allowing students to use the app, begin a discussion on ancient pottery. Use pictures from the Internet to display examples of pottery through the ages, including Roman, Greek, Aztec, Chinese, African, and Egyptian pottery.

> In pairs, have students follow the instructions given by a virtual customer to create a specific piece of pottery. Challenge students to get the highest star-rating possible.

> Have older students research the various ways pottery was made through the ages. Instruct them to make a historical time line to present their findings.

At Home

> Build your child's communication and listening skills by having him or her design pottery to fit your verbal specifications. Give directions to include various cultural art styles on the pottery.

> Access the shop portion of the app. Have your child choose a cultural pottery style they like best. Research that culture on the Internet or at the library with your child. Then, using the app, have him or her design a pot that matches that cultural style.

> After using *Let's create! Pottery*, find a community art class that will allow your child to use a real potter's wheel to create cultural art.

Geographia

CILAT

Suggested Grades
4–8

Available
iTunes

Description

With its bright colors and engaging graphics, this app provides a fun and easy way to learn the names of the states and their capitals. The states are grouped by regions of the country to make learning more focused. The audio feature praises correct responses and encourages children to try again for responses that are incorrect. *Geographia* includes the following key features:

> Options for single or additional players

> Rewards for correctly answered questions

> A scoring chart for each player that tracks the states and capitals they have learned and those that need more practice

At School

> Place this app in a center and allow students to study states and state capitals.

> In a whole-group instructional setting, connect your mobile device to a projector. Have the class practice naming the states together, Jeopardy-style. First, divide students into teams. Have teams take turns choosing which region to study first. Then, say "This is the state capital of...." Point at the state. Have students answer "What is...," and say the name of the state's capital. The team with the most correct answers wins.

> Use the scoring chart to assess a student's progress and provide a study partner for those who need extra help or motivation.

At Home

> Encourage your child to practice one region until they have mastered all of the states and capitals in that region. Then, have your child practice the next region.

> Have your child research other facts about the states and capitals, such as state birds and flowers, or famous buildings in capital cities.

> After using *Geographia*, make a game of quizzing your child on the state capitals of a region as you are riding in the car, standing in line at the grocery store, or waiting for an appointment.

Geo Walk HD-3D World Fact Book

Vito Technology Inc.

Suggested Grades
4–8

Available
iTunes

Description

Spin the globe to a part of the world you want to explore, or search for one using the category filter. What fits in the palm of your hand, is furry, and has wings? A bumblebee bat, of course! That's just one of 500 unusual animals, insects, places, people, architectural structures, and plants that are waiting for you to discover. *Geo Walk HD-3D World Fact Book* includes the following key features:

> Two viewing modes

> No Internet connection required

> Multiple-choice quizzes

> Sharing with email, Facebook, and Twitter™

At School

> In pairs, have younger students access the app's globe mode. Send students on a scavenger hunt to locate a list of animals, insects, and places that are found around the world. Give students clues to help them search in the correct part of the world. Have them write three facts about each item on their lists.

> Place this app in a center and allow students to explore the app to learn fascinating trivia about the world. Tell them to keep a list of the discoveries they make. At the end of the session, have them research two or three of their discoveries to collect more information.

> In small groups, have students plan a trip around the world. Ask them to keep a log of the interesting architectural structures, animals, or places they want to see in person after using the app. Then, have students create itineraries for the places they would like to visit the most. Have them present their itineraries to the class.

At Home

> Explore the various articles and pictures in this app. Encourage your child to explore a part of the world he or she wants to know more about.

> Help your child search for famous landmarks, places, or animals you have already seen in person. Have your child name what he or she knows about a place before reading the back of the picture.

HistoryTools

Belling Productions Inc

Suggested Grades
4–12

Available
iTunes

Description

Discover what happened in history on each day of the year. The app opens to the current date and lists famous births and deaths, interesting historical trivia, and events in all industries including art, politics, media, inventions, crime, discoveries, and sports. *HistoryTools* includes the following key features:

> Over 5,700 events, 6,200 birthdays, 4,000 deaths, and 600 holidays

> Option to enter and save your own events

> Events searchable by date and keywords

At School

> Place this app in a center and allow students to read famous historical events and happenings that took place on the current date.

> Divide the class into groups, and have students sign up for one of the events that happened on this day in history. Tell students to research that event, print pictures, and create a presentation. Allow time for students to present to the class.

> Choose one event in history from the current date, and have students work together to determine how this event, invention, or the birth or death of a certain person shaped and changed history.

> Challenge students to have an open discussion about the events that happened on a certain date. Encourage them to share their knowledge about each event. Correct any misconceptions, and add your own insights to the conversation.

At Home

> Encourage your child to select an event from the current date to discuss with your family. Encourage family members to answer your child's questions and add additional information.

> Work with your child to add important family events, milestones, and birthdays to the app.

> On a family member's birthday, read the day's event with your child, and help him or her select special events that can be added to a birthday card.

© Shell Education

History:Maps of World

Seung-Bin Cho

Suggested Grades
4–12

Available
iTunes

Description

This collection of historical maps is for the explorers at heart. It includes maps showing geography from The Roman Empire to United States political maps from the 1970s. This anthology is an asset to every history class. *History:Maps of World* includes the following key features:

› Over 150 maps through the centuries, organized by category or era

› Zoom in and out

› Keyword search

At School

› Place this app in a center and allow students to explore the different maps. Have them write three observations about the maps and share them with a classmate.

› In pairs, assign students a map. Instruct them to conduct additional research on world events at the time of the map's relevance. Have students prepare a presentation to teach the class about the map and its importance. Ask students to consider the events that helped shape the geography of the map, whether the map is an accurate representation of the world today, and why some areas of the map are blank.

› In a whole-group instructional setting, connect your mobile device to a projector. Display a map that will supplement your lesson plans.

At Home

› Have your child choose a map. Let your child explain what he or she understands about the map, and add to the discussion by sharing your knowledge.

› Work with your child to compare maps of a particular continent. For example, study the maps of Europe from A.D. 912, 1135, 1730, 1740, 1810, 1815, and present day. Help your child find similarities and differences between the maps and encourage them to consider what events occurred to cause a change in the geography on the map.

› After using *History:Maps of World* with your child, have him or her research how maps are made.

Presidents vs. Aliens

Dan Russell-Pinson

Suggested Grades
4–12

Available
iTunes

Description

The presidents of the United States need your help! Defeat the invading aliens as you learn about all United States presidents. The more trivia questions you answer correctly, the more presidents you can fling at the aliens to knock them down! Collect as many presidents as possible for your personalized screen, unlocking two more exciting bonus games along the way: *Heads of State!* and *Executive Order! Presidents vs. Aliens* includes the following key features:

> Filters questions to suit grade level

> 44 president flash cards

> Hundreds of unique questions

At School

> Place this app in a center and allow students to strengthen their knowledge of the presidents' appearances, political parties, predecessors and successors, nicknames, quotes, general facts, and historical events.

> Have students study the presidential flash cards before they play. Then, have them play the app independently or in pairs.

> In a whole-group instructional setting, connect your mobile device to a projector. Guide your students through several trivia questions while discussing deductive reasoning and how to use the process of elimination to help them choose the correct answer.

At Home

> Read the trivia questions to or with your child. Before tapping the answer to a question, ask your child to explain his or her reasons for making that choice.

> Encourage your child to share his or her knowledge about the presidents. Have your child write a letter to a president of his or her choice telling what he or she has learned about him.

> Promote teamwork between siblings by having them work together. Instruct the older sibling to answer trivia questions and the younger sibling to fling presidents at the aliens.

© Shell Education

Stack the Countries

Dan Russell-Pinson

Suggested Grades
4–12

Available
iTunes

Description

Stack the Countries will make you an expert in country capitals, languages, and shapes in no time! Answer the fun trivia questions correctly to stack a country. Stack them to the checkered line, and you will win a country to add to your own personalized and interactive map. Collect as many countries as possible, unlocking two more exciting bonus games along the way: *Map It!* and *Pile up! Stack the Countries* includes the following key features:

> Flash cards for studying country trivia

> Countries scaled to size relative to one another

> Realistic physics engine

> Pictures of famous landmarks around the world

> Option to play in English, Spanish, and French

At School

> Place this app in a center and allow students to strengthen their knowledge of country capitals, shapes, landmarks, languages, locations, and bordering countries.

> In pairs, direct students to take turns answering trivia questions and reviewing the country flash cards.

> In a whole-group instructional setting, connect your mobile device to a projector. Divide the class into groups and provide each group with a dry-erase board and marker. Display a trivia question and have groups discuss and choose an answer to the question. Then, have them write their answer on dry-erase boards. The first group to give five correct answers wins.

At Home

> Read the trivia questions to or with your child. Give pointers to help him or her stack the countries most effectively to reach the checkered line.

> Review the app's flash cards with your child before playing the game.

> Have your child test your knowledge of countries, allowing him or her to be the teacher and you the student.

Stack the States

Dan Russell-Pinson

Suggested Grades
4–12

Available
iTunes

Description

Stack the States will make you an expert in state capitals, abbreviations, and shapes in no time! Answer the fun trivia questions correctly to stack a state. Stack them to the checkered line, and you will win a state to add to your own personalized and interactive map. Collect all 50 states, unlocking three more exciting bonus games along the way: *Pile up!*, *Puzzler*, and *Capital Drop*. *Stack the States* includes the following key features:

> Flash cards for studying state trivia

> States scaled to size relative to one another

> Realistic physics engine

> Pictures of famous United States landmarks

At School

> Place this app in a center and allow students to strengthen their knowledge of United States state capitals, shapes, landmarks, nicknames, abbreviations, locations, and bordering states.

> In pairs, direct students to take turns answering trivia questions and reviewing the state flash cards.

> In a whole-group instructional setting, connect your mobile device to a projector. Divide the class into groups and provide each group with a dry-erase board and marker. Display the trivia question, allowing groups time to decide on the correct answer and write it on their dry-erase board. The first group to give 10 correct answers wins.

At Home

> Read the trivia questions to or with your child. Give your child pointers to help him or her stack the states most effectively to reach the checkered line.

> Review the flash cards with your child before playing the game.

> Have your child test your knowledge on U.S. states, allowing him or her to be the teacher and you the student.

European Exploration: The Age of Discovery

GAMeS Lab at RU

Suggested Grades
4–12

Available
iTunes

Description

It is the 15th century, and you are in charge of the expedition to the New World! Start your adventure into the unknown by preparing for the journey. Hire a famous explorer, build a ship, buy supplies, and set sail to make important discoveries around the globe! The high seas is a dangerous place, so stand guard. *European Exploration: The Age of Discovery* includes the following key features:

> Realistic simulation of exploration of the New World

> Game tutorial

> Game progress page

> Information on explorers

At School

> In a whole-group instructional setting with younger students, connect your mobile device to a projector. Demonstrate how to use the game. Begin an expedition together so students know what to expect when they play independently or in pairs.

> In pairs, have students work together to explore the app. Tell them to keep a list of the discoveries they make. At the end of the session, have them use the Internet to research two of their discoveries. Ask students if the explorer they chose in the game truly made the discovery in the past.

> Lead students in a discussion about world exploration in the 15th century. Ask students to consider the impact this exploration had on the world.

At Home

> As you set off on an expedition with your child, tell him or her to watch the time pass in the bottom-right corner of the screen. Ask him or her if a short amount of time or a large amount of time is passing as the ship sails. Explain that ships used to spend months at sea, much longer than ships that travel the seas today!

> After using *European Exploration: The Age of Discovery* with your child, have him or her research life aboard a ship during the 15th century. Find books, watch movies, and search the Internet to learn more about the Spanish explorers of the 15th century.

The Civil War Today

A&E Television Networks Mobile

Suggested Grades
5–8

Available
iTunes

Description

Read about the Civil War as it unfolded. How did the Civil War begin? How did it end? Find out over a four year period as this app tracks a day-by-day recount of the war. Each day, a new interactive newspaper will appear, including pictures of famous historical figures, interactive quizzes, a growing casualty list, and behind the scenes information about colonial life. *The Civil War Today* includes the following key features:

> Thousands of original documents, photos, diary entries, and quotes to explore

> Daily updates starting April 12, 2011, and ending April 26, 2015, with daily information unfolding as it did 150 years ago

> Personal letters and diary entries from historical figures such as Abraham Lincoln and Horatio Nelson Taft

> Videos, searchable glossary, and biography section

At School

> In a whole-group instructional setting, connect your mobile device to a projector. Help students understand the events leading up to the Civil War by reading the "Prelude to War" entry at the beginning of the time line. Ask students to summarize the conflicts between the Northern and Southern states. Have students infer whether most people were aware that a war was developing.

> In teacher-led small groups, have students explore the background scenes that depict day-to-day life for farmers, soldiers, plantation and rail workers, and others. Ask students how the Civil War might have been different if it had occurred today.

> In pairs, have students review the biographies of prominent figures, such as Abraham Lincoln and Ulysses S. Grant. Have them select one person to research their involvement in and stance on the Civil War.

At Home

> Challenge your child to infer what he or she may read in the daily installment. Then, read the daily updates with your child. Ask your child to share his or her thoughts about the events that occurred and their effects on the people of the time.

> Take the interactive quiz with your child and discuss the answers.

© Shell Education

Constitution

Clint Bagwell Consulting

Suggested Grades

5–12

Note: Includes advertisements

Available

iTunes

Description

Read the entire text of the United States Constitution along with short biographies on the founding fathers who signed it. Then, get an up-close look at a famous painting depicting the day the Constitution was signed. The *Declaration* app is also available from Clint Bagwell Consulting. *Constitution* includes the following key features:

> Full text of the United States Constitution, with notes about each amendment

> Painting of *Scene at the Signing of the Constitution of the United States* by Howard Chandler Christy

> Background information about each signer

At School

> Place this app in a center and allow students to refer to it as they complete class assignments or homework.

> In a whole-group instructional setting, connect your mobile device to a projector. Discuss the history of the U.S. Constitution. Read the Preamble aloud. Help students analyze key phrases, such as "form a more perfect union," "establish justice," and "insure domestic tranquility."

> In teacher-led small groups, describe the students in class as a group of people who must work together, similar to the way each state in the United States must work together. Instruct students to draft a class constitution. Explain that they must come up with a list of rules to follow. Have them work together and write the rules on parchment paper and then sign the finished class constitution.

At Home

> Read the U.S. Constitution with your child. Explain what it represents and why it is important. Encourage family members to work with you and your child to create a family constitution to hang on a wall or on the refrigerator.

> Encourage your child to watch a public presidential address, listening for mentions of the U.S. Constitution. Ask your child why he or she thinks people still value the U.S. Constitution more than 200 years after it was written.

Virtual Tour to the Great Wall HD

516 Inc

Suggested Grades
6–8

Available
iTunes

Description

View the striking high-definition photographs of the Great Wall of China as serene music plays in the background. Then, read about the Jinshanling Great Wall, learning the history of one of the greatest wonders of the world. Save the photographs to use as screen backgrounds. *Virtual Tour of the Great Wall HD* includes the following key features:

> Auto-play Slide Show and Pause functions

> Detailed history page

> Diagram of the Great Wall of China, including important tower names

At School

> Before using the app, have a discussion with students about the events that led up to the construction of the Great Wall of China.

> In a whole-group instructional setting, connect your mobile device to a projector. Allow the images to play automatically as you teach about the Great Wall of China. Distribute art supplies to students, and have them build a model of one section of the Great Wall.

> Divide the class into groups and have students use this app to select a part of the Great Wall to research. Instruct students to use the Internet or the school library to research stories about the people who worked on the wall and how long their portion of the wall took to complete. Have them present their findings to the class.

> Place this app in a center, and have students take turns reading aloud the app's historical passage about the Great Wall of China.

At Home

> Before using this app, work with your child to locate China on a map. Then, determine where the Great Wall of China is located, and trace its length on the map. Point out that it is over 2,414 km (1,500 mi.) long, which is longer than many rivers of the world.

> Read the historical passage with your child. Encourage your child to ask you questions about what they have read. Summarize difficult passages, if needed.

 #50847—110 Amazing Apps for Education © Shell Education

TimeTours: Chichen Itza

Martin Gruhn &
Bernfried Eisenblätter

Suggested Grades
6–12

Available
iTunes

Description

Experience the ancient Mayan civilization with this app as you explore Chichen Itza through an illustrated map. Enjoy the rich historical information in the form of pictures, text, 3-D representations, and panoramic views. Use the map, or tap the top-right-hand corner of the home screen for more options. *TimeTours: Chichen Itza* includes the following key features:

> 3-D reconstructions of site landmarks

> Now and Then comparisons

> Maps showing how to get to Chichen Itza from your location

> News about excavation and information about nearby historical hotels

At School

> In a whole-group instructional setting, connect your mobile device to a projector. Use this app as a supplement to your lessons about the Mayan civilization. Display the Now & Then images. Then, have students discuss the similarities and differences between the images. Discuss other aspects of the Mayan culture that are of interest to students.

> In teacher-led small groups, have students learn about this ancient civilization and compare the Mayan structures to the ones we build today.

> Have students write a research paper on Chichen Itza. Examples of suggested topics include the surrounding geography; the purposes of each structure and what that reveals about the Mayan culture; and a description of the buildings, the artifacts, and the materials used to construct the city.

At Home

> Use the Find Target feature to map the route you and your child would take on a trip to Chichen Itza. Research other historical sites in Mexico you will pass or explore on your journey.

> After exploring the app, ask your child which place he or she would want to investigate on a trip to Chichen Itza and why.

HISTORY™ Egypt HD

Slitherine

Suggested Grades
6–12

Available
iTunes

Description

As the leader of your people, it is up to you to bring the Egyptian Empire to the height of its power. In this interactive history-based app, develop an army to expand your empire into new regions through war or friendship, trade, commerce, and architecture while also strengthening political power and economic growth. *HISTORY Egypt HD* includes the following key features:

> Nine historic campaigns to complete with varying objectives

> 50 buildings to construct

> Multiplayer option

At School

> In a whole-group instructional setting, connect your mobile device to a projector. Facilitate a discussion about the rise of the Egyptian empire. Direct students to view the app. Explain the game objectives and how students can review their progress. Then, work with students to generate specific strategies that could help them build an empire.

> Use this app as a supplement to a history lesson. Encourage a discussion with students about how this app mirrors Egyptian history.

> In pairs, have students work together to build an empire. Or, play in Multiplayer mode. Discuss the four civilizations listed under Diplomacy: Macedonians, Babylonians, Persians, and Assyrians. Instruct students to conduct general research on each group. Also, have students refer to a map that shows where these places were located in relation to one another.

At Home

> Use this app to motivate your child to learn about Egyptian history. Ask your child questions, such as whether each civilization mentioned in the app existed, where each was located, and when each empire was at its height. Encourage your child to find answers to these questions.

> Play the game in Multiplayer mode, or work together to conquer and build your Egyptian empire!

© Shell Education

Virtual History ROMA

Arnoldo Mondadori Editore S.p.A.

Suggested Grades
6–12

Available
iTunes

Description

With its amazing features and historical content, *Virtual History ROMA* brings ancient Rome to life. This richly detailed app conveniently organizes its content around an easy-to-use index that leads to information about all aspects of the Roman Empire, such as its military conquests, art, and everyday life. *Virtual History ROMA* includes the following key features:

> Interactive models of structures and places around Rome

> Comparisons that show how Rome looked throughout time

At School

> Place this app in a center and allow students enough time to read the detailed information on the Roman Empire and enjoy the virtual tour.

> Divide the class into groups and instruct students to use the app's index as a guide as they find the answers to a series of questions you provide. Have them record their answers on a separate sheet of paper. Provide each group with a different set of questions. Have groups share their answers with the class.

> In a whole-group instructional setting, encourage a discussion of the Roman Empire. Have students form generalizations about the Roman culture and civilization based on what they read in the app.

At Home

> Use the index to guide you and your child through ancient Rome. Allow him or her to start the virtual tour by selecting a topic that sounds most interesting.

> Challenge your child to discover facts about Rome, using the different features of this app. Discuss with your child what he or she thinks was important to the ancient Romans. Ask your child if he or she would have enjoyed living in ancient Rome and why.

MyCongress

ObjectiveApps, LLC

Suggested Grades
9–12

Available
iTunes

Description

Use *MyCongress* to find the contact information of elected United States Congressional officials. Read their work and educational biographies, and follow RSS feeds to receive recent news, including YouTube videos and Twitter updates. *MyCongress* includes the following key features:

> Searchable list of United States Congressional officials

> Direct contact details and links to websites

> Bookmarks

At School

> Before using the app, review the responsibilities of senators and representatives with your students.

> In a whole-group instructional setting, connect your mobile device to a projector. Display the Home Screen page of the app. Type in your school's zip code to locate the United States Congressional officials that are in your geographic area. Write the names of these officials on the board so students can refer to them later.

> Place this app in a center, and have students get the latest news on the United States Congressional officials in their area. Instruct students to choose one topic from the official's latest news feed. Direct them to research this topic and then write a letter to the official with suggestions, questions, or opinions about it.

At Home

> Have your child use the app to learn about your state's Congressional officials. Encourage your child to write to either a state senator or representative about an issue that is important to him or her. Help your child by reviewing his or her letter to make sure it is clear and concise, and assisting in revising the letter, if necessary.

> Work with your child to research what steps are needed to become a United States Congressional official. Ask your child if this is the type of career he or she would like to pursue, and if so, what kind of education and work experience is needed.

Amazing Cross-Curricular Apps

How I Use My Apps

Fish School

Duck Duck Moose, Partnership

Suggested Grades
Pre-K–K

Available
iTunes

Description

Welcome to *Fish School*! Children will love watching the colorful schools of fish arrange themselves into numbers, shapes, colors, and letters. With eight educational activities to choose from, children will be singing their ABCs and recognizing shapes, letters, and numbers in no time! *Fish School* includes the following key features:

> Teaches numbers from 1 to 20

> A memory game to practice shape, size, and color

> Playtime with fish and other sea creatures

> An engaging version of the *Alphabet Song*, including Mozart variations performed in violin and cello

At School

> Place this app in a center and allow students to complete the activities.

> In pairs, have students jump ahead to the Difference page. Instruct them to take turns tapping the fish that doesn't belong in the school.

> In a whole-group instructional setting, connect your mobile device to a projector. Display the *Alphabet Song* page, and instruct the class to sing along with the music.

At Home

> Show your child how to swipe the fish to move forward and backward as he or she learns letters, numbers, and shapes.

> Use the Playtime page to teach your child the difference between big and small. Hold your finger on a fish to make it double in size.

> After using *Fish School*, work with your child to spot the letters, numbers, and shapes in favorite books and on signs and buildings in the world around you.

Super Stretch Yoga

The Adventures of
Super Stretch, LLC

Suggested Grades
Pre-K–5

Available
iTunes

Description

Learn to balance, breathe, and move by joining Super Stretch and his friends in a fun yoga adventure. Practice 12 yoga poses that are demonstrated by real children and colorful animations. Collect a star for each yoga pose in order to take a team photo! *Super Stretch Yoga* includes the following key features:

> Refreshing music for each pose

> Breathing techniques for relaxation

> Appealing graphics mixed with live-action footage

At School

> In a whole-group instructional setting, connect your mobile device to a projector. Clear space in the classroom for students to spread out. Select the Play All feature to allow students to complete all 12 poses.

> In pairs, have older students research the general health benefits that can be gained from making yoga a part of their exercise regimen.

> In a teacher-led small group, encourage a discussion about how yoga relaxes the mind and body. Have students define stress. Ask them if children can get stressed, too. Have them share a time when they felt stress. Brainstorm with students to determine ways that will help them cope with stress, such as deep breathing and yoga.

At Home

> Motivate your child about exercise and yoga by practicing all 12 yoga poses with him or her.

> After you have completed all 12 poses, take a team photo with your child.

> After using *Super Stretch Yoga*, spend time with your child researching additional beginning yoga moves.

Mobicip Safe Browser

Mobicip, LLC

Suggested Grades
K–8

Available
iTunes, Google Play

Description

This is the perfect app for teachers and parents who want surfing the Internet to be a safe and fun experience for their children. Benefit from this state-of-the-art content filtering engine that blocks out offensive and inappropriate Internet sites. *Mobicip Safe Browser* includes the following key features:

> Easy-to-use web browser

> Filters based on age, as well as automatic filtering used by school systems

> Safe searching, which cannot be disabled

> YouTube filter

> Internet activity tracking

> Option to build your own filter

At School

> Place this app in a center and allow students to surf the Web during free time.

> In pairs, have students use *Mobicip Safe Browser* to complete a research project.

> In a whole-group instructional setting, connect your mobile device to a projector. Facilitate a discussion about Internet safety and why it is important to take safety precautions when using the Internet. Show students the different ways *Mobicip Safe Browser* can filter information. Then, have students write a journal entry on the importance of Internet safety.

At Home

> Allow your child to use this app to explore the Internet at his or her own leisure.

> Encourage your child to use the app to look up answers to questions that come into everyday conversation. For example, if your family is discussing which day of the week a holiday falls on, ask your child to look up the date using the browser.

Google Earth

Google Mobile

Suggested Grades
K–12

Available
iTunes, Google Play

Description

Google Earth zips you around the globe without ever leaving home. Explore Earth through global satellite and high-resolution aerial imagery. Zoom in on famous landmarks, get directions, or browse geo-located photos and Wikipedia articles. *Google Earth* includes the following key features:

› Current Location marker

› Keyword search for cities, businesses, and famous landmarks

› Option to explore layers such as places, businesses, and photos

At School

› Place this app in a center and allow students to become familiar with the app's features. Have students search for their house, local businesses, and their current location.

› In pairs, send students on a scavenger hunt to locate a list of famous landmarks. Have students write what they discover about each landmark using geo-located photos and articles that are provided.

› In pairs, have students research geological features, such as volcanoes, canyons, mountain ranges, and oceans. Have them write a description of what these geological features look like in *Google Earth*.

› In small groups, have students use *Google Earth* to plan a trip around the world. Ask them to keep a log of the places they will visit, including museums, hotels, amusement parks, and landmarks. Have them present their itineraries to the class.

At Home

› Have your child explore this app and then share with you the features he or she has discovered.

› Help your child locate the places you visit regularly, such as school, home, the grocery store, and other local businesses. Look for new places to visit in your community.

› Plan a family vacation with your child using this app. Explore several possible locations, researching nearby attractions, hotels, and restaurants.

DINOSAURS: The American Museum of Natural History Collections

American Museum of Natural History

Suggested Grades
K–12

Available
iTunes

Description

Take a look at the museum with the world's largest collection of dinosaur fossils! View a mosaic of a Tyrannosaurus rex composed of hundreds of photos from the museum's archives. It includes photographs of actual fossils, excavation sites, and artistic interpretations of what the dinosaurs may have looked like in their original habitat. *DINOSAURS: The American Museum of Natural History Collections* includes the following key features:

> ❭ T-Rex mosaic made from hundreds of photos

> ❭ Information about each dinosaur fossil, including the scientific name, the age, and the location of the fossil discovery and excavation date

At School

> ❭ In a whole-group instructional setting, connect your mobile device to a projector. Show students your favorite photos from the app's virtual collection. Lead a discussion about how these finds changed our understanding of Earth.

> ❭ Place this app in a center and allow students to discuss the similarities and differences among the dinosaurs in the exhibits. Have students write about their favorite picture and what it represents.

> ❭ If available, bring in fossils from a nature center or teacher's science center to inspire further scientific study and discussion.

At Home

> ❭ Have your child tap on the pictures of the mosaic to enlarge them. Talk about the pictured fossils and the excavation sites, as well as speculate about the lives of paleontologists.

> ❭ Have an older child act as a museum docent, and guide a younger family member though the app's exhibits.

> ❭ After using *DINOSAURS: The American Museum of Natural History Collections* with your child, plan a fossil dig by hiding objects on a tray or in a box and covering them with sand or earth. Then, have your child dig to find the objects. Afterward, talk about the excitement paleontologists may feel when they discover fossils.

JumpStart Jetpack

Knowledge Adventure

Suggested Grades
1–3

Available
iTunes

Description

Manipulate a jetpack character through a mixture of correct and incorrect answers to language arts and math questions. Collect as many points as possible by collecting the correct answers and zapping away the incorrect ones. *JumpStart Jetpack* includes the following key features:

> Three curriculum levels with game difficulty settings at each level

> Language arts concepts, such as parts of speech, word endings, and word classification

> Mathematics concepts, such as counting, shapes, addition, subtraction, multiplication, and division

> A game tutorial

> Left-handed joystick option

At School

> In a whole-group instructional setting, connect the mobile device to a projector. Demonstrate how to use the app. Then, have students write instructions of how to play the game.

> Place this app in a center and tell students which curriculum level to use. Allow them to select a language arts or mathematics game to play. Monitor their progress, and adjust the curriculum level if necessary.

> Have students play levels that supplement what they are currently learning.

> Encourage students to choose progressively harder difficulty settings as they master the language arts and math skills presented in the app.

At Home

> Help your child figure out the controls and the object of the game. Choose levels that correspond with what your child is learning in school. Then, have fun playing each level with your child.

> Challenge your child to repeat a game to improve a high score or to play a more difficult level.

Khan Academy

Khan Academy

Suggested Grades
K–12

Available
iTunes

Description

With access to over 2,700 videos, *Khan Academy* provides you with the exploratory educational experience. This extensive video library covers a wide range of topics to satisfy even the most curious minds. Browse the long list of categories, including math, physics, chemistry, art history, finance, and more. *Khan Academy* includes the following key features:

> Downloadable videos

> Video subtitles

> A user account to track achievements

At School

> After watching a video, divide the class into groups of four. Have each group compose a list of questions they had about the video. Have groups exchange question lists and then work as a group to answer the questions. Have a group discussion sharing the answers when groups have finished.

> Create a class blog about *Khan Academy*. Have students work in pairs to write video reviews, including star ratings. Work with them to create a flyer about their blog to hand out to teachers and students at your school.

> Place this app in a center and allow students to watch a video of their choice from a list provided by the teacher. Have them write a short summary of each video he or she watched.

At Home

> Assist your child in choosing a video that corresponds to the subject of his or her homework. Watch the video together and discuss how the topic relates to what he or she is currently learning.

> Set a goal with your child to watch one video a day. Work with your child to devise a rating system to rate each video. Discuss rating criteria with your child and why each video received a specific rating. Create a chart to track your progress and record your ratings. Have your child encourage family members to use the chart to select videos to watch together.

BrainPOP Featured Movie

BrainPop®

Suggested Grades
3–6

Available
iTunes

Description

Watch a new and *free* animated movie every day! Or, tap the **MORE BRAINPOP** button to watch past movies you may have missed. Then, take the interactive quiz to test your knowledge. Movie topics cover everything from DNA to digital animation to the Civil War. *BrainPOP Featured Movie* includes the following key features:

> Curriculum-based movie categories, including Science, Math, Social Studies, English, Technology, Engineering, Arts & Music, and Health

> Captioned movies

> Option to archive quiz scores

> BrainPOP website with corresponding activity pages, lesson plans, and more

At School

> Place this app in a center and allow students to watch the daily movie and take the quiz independently or as a group.

> In pairs, instruct students to choose a movie, take the quiz, and complete additional research on the movie topic. Have them present their research to the class.

> In a whole-group instructional setting, connect your mobile device to a projector. Display a movie as an introduction to a lesson. Corresponding lesson plans and activities can be found on BrainPOP's website.

At Home

> Watch the daily movie with your child. Encourage your child to discuss what he or she has learned from the daily movie.

> Have your child write what he or she thinks is the main idea of a movie. Then, have your child draw a picture or diagram to illustrate the main idea.

     © Shell Education

Library Of Congress— Virtual Tour

Library of Congress

Suggested Grades
4–12

Available
iTunes

Description

If you have never been to the Library of Congress, this great app will take you there! Tap the **EXPLORE** button and sample these selections: The Main Reading Room, The Great Hall, Exploring the Early Americas, Creating the United States, The Bible Collection, Thomas Jefferson Library, and Minerva. *Library Of Congress—Virtual Tour* includes the following key features:

> Audio file containing audio information for each room

> A camera, which provides a close-up view of the displayed artifacts, maps, and documents

> Related links for more information

At School

> In a whole-group instructional setting, encourage a discussion about the Library of Congress. Have students tell you why they think this library was created and why it is important to keep a documented record of our history.

> Place this app in a center, and allow students time to read about the Library of Congress. Ask them to write what impressed them the most about the Library of Congress. Then, ask which room they would visit first if they were to take a trip to the physical Library of Congress in Washington, DC and why.

> In pairs, have students listen to the audio file and then discuss with their partner what feelings and thoughts they had after listening. Have them discuss what surprised them and why.

At Home

> Explore the Library of Congress with your child, exchanging comments on the exhibitions. Ask your child what he or she finds most interesting and would like to know more about. Encourage your child to research that topic in the library or on the Internet.

> Lead a discussion with your child about which room is his or her favorite and why.

> Encourage your child to connect prior knowledge of American history to what he or she has observed on the virtual tour.

Back in Time

LANDKA

Suggested Grades
5–12

Available
iTunes

Description

Back in Time takes you on an exciting trip back millions of years to the time of the Big Bang! Starting at the beginning of time, work your way through major events that occurred in our universe and on our planet up to the present day. The fascinating pictures, graphics, and animations are visually stunning and wonderful motivators for learning. *Back in Time* includes the following key features:

> Hundreds of interesting facts presented in an appealing way

> Beautiful illustrations, images, and animations

> Illustrated time lines

At School

> In a whole-group instructional setting, connect your mobile device to a projector. Display the Introduction page and ask for volunteers to read the text. Discuss how this app is an analogy and provide examples of other analogies. Ask students how the 24-hour analogy can help them understand the age of the universe.

> In small groups, have students create a time line listing the major events detailed in the app. Designate a particular time frame for each group. Instruct each group member to choose an event to write about and illustrate. Have them hang their illustration and drawing in the appropriate place on the time line. After the time line is complete, have each student present to the class his or her contribution to the time line and explain the significance of the event they chose.

At Home

> Have your child turn the clock as you explore the various time periods together.

> Discuss the images and read the text together. Clarify any event your child doesn't understand. Ask him or her *Who, What, When, Where,* and *Why* questions to build comprehension skills.

> After using *Back in Time*, take your child to the library to find additional information on a topic you both particularly enjoyed learning about.

                                    © Shell Education

Amazing Logic Puzzler Apps

How I Use My Apps

KickBox

MIND Research Institute

Suggested Grades
K–8

Available
iTunes

Description

Help Jiji the penguin by positioning lasers and mirrors to hit the balls out of his path. This fun and colorful thinking game begins with easy levels that become increasingly more challenging. Think you're becoming a *KickBox* pro? Check out the comprehensive graph that tracks your progress. *KickBox* includes the following key features:

> Seven progressive levels

> Problem solving without words

> Time bonuses for quick thinking

> Multi-player profiles

At School

> In a whole-group instructional setting, connect your mobile device to a projector and ask students to describe what they see and what they think is the goal of the game. Encourage students to press the **Go** button before attempting a puzzle so that they can determine in what direction the laser shoots. Ask for volunteers to help you complete the first few puzzles.

> Place this app in a center and have students take turns placing mirror pieces into the puzzle to help create a path for Jiji.

> In pairs, have students discuss what strategies they think they will help them solve each puzzle.

At Home

> Work with your child through the intro level of the app.

> Take turns manipulating the game and giving advice. Discuss the pitfalls you encounter, and the strategies you find most useful. Discuss what works and what doesn't as you play the game together.

> Organize a *KickBox* family competition. Challenge family members to complete challenging levels. Time how long it takes them to complete the levels, as well as how many times they have to restart the level. The person who completes it fastest with the least amount of tries wins!

Geared

Bryan Mitchell

Suggested Grades
K–12

Available
iTunes, Google Play

Description

Build a bridge of spinning gears in order to connect to the gear on the opposite side of the screen. Gears come in various sizes and colors, but without careful planning, you'll never make it to the other side! This logic puzzle will keep you busy for hours. *Geared* includes the following key features:

> Over 200 levels of varying difficulty from easy to extremely challenging

> Auto-save

> Level Editor for creating your own challenges

At School

> In a whole-group instructional setting with younger students, connect the mobile device to a projector. Complete several levels with students until they understand the goal of the game. Then, have students work in pairs to create, on paper, their own *Geared* puzzle.

> Have students research how gears work to learn more about the mechanical process and also help them become a more successful game player.

> Place this app in a center and have students solve the puzzles. After they master several levels, allow students to use the Level Editor to create their own games to play. Have students challenge others to solve the puzzle they created.

> In teacher-led small groups, help students develop a strategy when tackling difficult levels. Have them write a list of hints that will help them when completing a level.

At Home

> Discuss the goal of the game with your child and review the features together. Have your child complete a few levels while explaining his or her strategy for each one. Solve difficult levels together, one person moving the gears and the other giving strategy support.

> Organize a *Geared* family competition. Challenge family members to design their own levels. You and your child can vote on the most difficult level and most creative level. Award the winners with a special prize.

 © Shell Education

Amazing Alex HD

Rovio Entertainment Ltd.

Suggested Grades
K–12

Available
iTunes, Google Play, Amazon

Description

Amazing Alex needs your help to build some crazy contraptions! Use slingshots, skateboards, RC trucks and helicopters, darts, and other toys to solve each entertaining puzzle. If you are feeling extra inventive, build your own contraptions for your friends to solve. Better yet, challenge your friends to see who can be the most creative! *Amazing Alex HD* includes the following key features:

> Clues on how to solve each physics-based puzzle

> 100 levels, with a Level Editor for helping you build your own contraptions

> Share contraptions and puzzle solutions online

> Additional user-created puzzles for download

At School

> Place this app in a center and allow students to work together to solve the puzzles. Assign specific roles within the group, such as one student to read directions, one person to manipulate the screen, and others to suggest puzzle solutions.

> In pairs, instruct students to take turns designing a puzzle for the other to solve.

> In a whole-group instructional setting, connect your mobile device to a projector. Play several levels as a class, discussing cause and effect. Follow up by building a Rube Goldberg-like contraption as a class.

At Home

> To strengthen problem-solving skills, have your child create multiple solutions for each puzzle.

> Encourage your child to build a puzzle for a family member to solve.

> Assist your child in building a Rube Goldberg-like contraption using household items and toys. Challenge each other to solve these real-life contraptions.

Rollercoaster Builder Travel

Dimension Technics

Suggested Grades
3–8

Available
iTunes

Description

Try your hand at building your very own roller coaster! Get the train from one side of the screen to the other without crashing. Try to collect all the gold coins as you roll through the levels. Watch a replay video of each completed level to show off your building skills. *Rollercoaster Builder Travel* includes the following key features:

> 30 roller coaster building puzzles with varied difficulty

> Seven lesson tutorials for tips and tricks

> Colorful and fun background of amusement parks

At School

> In a whole-group instructional setting, connect your mobile device to a projector. Discuss the physics of roller coasters, including how most roller coasters do not have engines. Use the app to supplement your lesson.

> Place this app in a center and have students complete the tutorial.

> In pairs, instruct students to take turns building a roller coaster. Direct one student to describe where to place the tracks while the other student draws it.

At Home

> Work with your child to build a rollercoaster that does not crash. Problem solve with him or her to determine ways to collect all the gold coins in each level.

> Watch online videos showing roller coasters. Ask your child to describe how the roller coaster is shaped. Ask what would happen if the track was steeper, less steep, or more curved.

> If possible, after using *Rollercoaster Builder Travel*, take your child to a local amusement park where he or she can ride a roller coaster. Then, discuss with your child how the roller coaster could be improved.

© Shell Education

Hanoi

NimbleBit LLC

Suggested Grades
3–12

Available
iTunes

Description

Move a tower of discs from the left side of the screen to the right. Using logic to manipulate the discs, you must move your tower by stacking smaller discs only on top of larger ones. This child-friendly game allows for trial and error as you plan out your moves. *Hanoi* includes the following key features:

> Discs added in new levels to increase difficulty

> Touch and slide controls

At School

> In a whole-group instructional setting, connect your mobile device to a projector. Explain the goal of the game to the class as you demonstrate how to play.

> According to the independent level of your students, allow them to work in small groups, pairs, or individually. Have students discover and discuss the strategies necessary to move the discs to the right side of the screen.

> In teacher-led small groups, choose a level, and ask your students to plan several steps ahead before actually moving the discs. Have students verbalize the steps that are needed to solve the puzzle.

> Challenge students to repeat a level and reduce the amount of moves or time it takes to solve the puzzle.

At Home

> Discuss the goal of the game with your child, and help him or her discover how the discs move.

> See if you and your child can plan out a few steps before moving the discs. Encourage your child to verbalize what steps need to be taken and why.

> Challenge your child to explain the best strategies for completing each level.

World of Goo

2D BOY

Suggested Grades
3–12

Available
iTunes, Google Play

Description

The *World of Goo* is populated by none other than the quirky and curious globs of goo that are thrilled to work together to form bridges, structures, cannonballs, a giant tongue, and more! Follow the goo ball's exciting story line in each colorfully animated level. *World of Goo* includes the following key features:

> Save game option for up to three players

> Dynamic and entertaining graphics

> Magical background music and fun sound effects

> Four chapters with multiple levels per chapter, and an epilogue

At School

> In teacher-led small groups, have students discuss why they must consider weight distribution and gravity while building their goo structures. Use this discussion as an introduction to a lesson on the physics of engineering and architecture.

> In pairs, instruct students to enter the World of Goo Corporation and see who can build the tallest tower, using the extra goo balls they have collected. Tell them that it does not count if their towers topple over.

> In a whole-group instructional setting, explain to students that they will be making towers using marshmallows and coffee stirrers. Divide students into groups of two or three. Provide 20 marshmallows per group and as many coffee stirrers as needed. Explain that the goal is to build the tallest tower without it toppling. Measure each group's complete tower to determine the winners.

At Home

> Assist younger children with reading the signs written by the Sign Painter.

> Encourage your child to explain his or her thought process when organizing the goo balls to form structures. Ask him or her to explain why the goo balls are placed where they are and what outcome is expected.

> Challenge your child to a *World of Goo* competition. Determine who can complete a level in the shortest amount of time and using the fewest goo balls.

Enigmo
Pangea Software, Inc.

Suggested Grades
3–12

Available
iTunes, Google Play, Amazon

Description

Earn points by using a variety of tools to redirect a flow of uncontrolled liquid into a vase. With each level of added difficulty, the player is given more tools and the opportunity to earn more points. *Enigmo* includes the following key features:

> 50 levels to solve with three different types of liquids to control

> Engineering parts that slide and rotate, such as bumpers, sliders, sponges and accelerators

> Level Editor for creating your own levels

At School

> In a whole-group instructional setting, connect the mobile device to a projector. Encourage students to explain what they see and what they think the object of the game is. Facilitate a discussion about the object of the game and the various tools that can be used to solve each puzzle.

> Place this app in a center, and have students solve the puzzles. After they master several levels, allow students to use the Level Editor to create their own games to play. Have students challenge others to solve the puzzle they created.

> Have older students design their own *Enigmo* contraption using objects found around the house and in the classroom. Tell students that, like the app, their object is to channel water into a vase. Allow them time outside to test their contraptions and make adjustments. Have them demonstrate their contraptions while standing in large plastic tubs to help conserve water.

At Home

> Take turns completing a level and have the observer give directions that will help solve the puzzle.

> Encourage your child to create a level using the Level Editor, and have him or her challenge you and other family members and friends to complete it.

> Organize an *Enigmo* family competition. Challenge family members to design their own levels. You and your child can vote on the most difficult level and most creative levels. Award the winners with a special prize.

Cut the Rope: Experiments

ZeptoLab UK Limited

Suggested Grades
4–12

Available
iTunes, Google Play, Amazon

Description

Om Nom is a little green monster with a huge appetite! Discovering Om Nom's craving for candy, the professor decides to experiment. Will you help the professor discover just how much candy Om Nom can eat? *Cut the Rope: Experiments* is a fun-filled logic game where you cut ropes to get the candy into Om Nom's mouth. *Cut the Rope: Experiments* includes the following key features:

> 75 experiment levels in three different settings

> Three level packs included

> Fun music and character sound effects

> Hidden images and extras

> Animated story line

At School

> In pairs, instruct students to take turns completing levels. Have them work together to find solutions to each level. Encourage students to replay the levels in which they do not receive all three stars.

> In teacher-led small groups, have students write out the steps they are going to take to solve a level before they attempt it. Alternatively, instruct students to trade their step-by-step directions with another student. Have students then solve the level to which their new set of directions corresponds.

> In a whole-group instructional setting, connect your mobile device to a projector. Display the first puzzle in this app. Walk students through solving a puzzle. Explain that it is acceptable to restart the level if they make a mistake. Encourage them to retrieve all three stars before moving on to a new level.

At Home

> Watch as your child completes levels, and offer help or praise when appropriate. Work together and discuss possible answers to more difficult levels.

> Encourage your child to explain his or her thought process as the level is being solved.

Boxed In-HD

Dennis Mengelt

Suggested Grades
4–12

Available
iTunes

Description

Your goal is to lead the robot to the exit, but first you have to use logic to push the boxes out of the way and get past the obstacles, including gates, switches, gears, and more. The crisp and colorful graphics make for an excellent game-play experience. *Boxed In-HD* includes the following key features:

> Levels of increasing difficulty

> Replay and Auto-save features

At School

> In a whole-group instructional setting, connect your mobile device to a projector. Demonstrate how to use the app, completing several levels as a class before having students attempt levels individually or in pairs.

> In pairs, instruct one student to move the robot while the other suggests solutions. Then, have them switch roles.

> In teacher-led small groups, have students write out the steps they are going to take to solve a level before they attempt it. Alternatively, instruct students to trade their step-by-step directions with another student. Have students then solve the new level.

At Home

> If your child is having difficulty, work with him or her in the beginning levels to demonstrate how to use the app and how to navigate the various elements in each level.

> Race against the clock with your child. See how many levels he or she can complete under 10 minutes. Challenge your child to beat his or her record.

> Encourage your child to explain his or her thought process while navigating each level. Discuss with your child the importance of planning out several steps in advance and why this is important to solving each puzzle.

Fantastic Contraption™

inXile Entertainment

Suggested Grades
4–12

Available
iTunes

Description

The object of *Fantastic Contraption* is to build a machine using the provided parts, and to get the "goal object" to move to the "goal area" of the screen. With multiple ways to solve each level, and a Level Editor to build your own levels, the fun never stops! *Fantastic Contraption 2* is also available from inXile Entertainment. *Fantastic Contraption* includes the following key features:

> Step-by-step tutorial

> 21 classic levels, 20 built-in puzzles, and over 16,000 downloadable levels

> Ability to share your contraptions online

> Ability to download user-made levels from around the world

At School

> In a whole-group instructional setting, connect your mobile device to a projector. Display the first puzzle in this app. Walk students through solving a puzzle. Have students work together to solve a few puzzles before attempting them on their own. Demonstrate how it is possible to solve a level in more than one way.

> In pairs, instruct students to work together to find multiple solutions to each level. Have pairs write a description of how to build a contraption for a particular level.

> In teacher-led small groups, have students build levels for other students to solve. Have each group build a level for you to solve. Encourage them to try to stump you with their level.

At Home

> To strengthen your child's problem-solving skills, have him or her explore to discover multiple solutions for each puzzle.

> Encourage your child to explain his or her thought process when organizing the objects to make a contraption. Ask him or her why they chose certain materials, why the pieces are placed where they are, and what outcome is expected.

> Work with your child to build a level for a family member to solve. Then, upload this level online for others around the world to enjoy.

Amazing
You Make It
Apps

How I Use My Apps

Toontastic

Launchpad Toys

Suggested Grades
Pre-K–5

Available
iTunes

Description

Let your creativity take flight and make your own animated cartoon stories with *Toontastic.* Record animations using *Toontastic's* extensive collection of characters or draw your own characters to animate. Record your own voice to narrate your story and add music to set the tone. *Toontastic* includes the following features:

> Story Arc storyboard helps you to plan the important scenes and plot points of the story (setup, conflict, challenge, climax, and resolution)

> Moveable characters to animate

> Multiple story settings to choose from

> Record function to narrate

> Multiple music settings that are driven by the emotion of each type of scene

> Sharing on ToonTube™, *Toontastic's* video sharing media site

At School

> Place this app in a center and allow students to become familiar with it. Have them create cartoons without instruction.

> In a whole-group instructional setting, connect your mobile device to a projector. Display the Story Arc page, and discuss the different parts of a story, such as setup, conflict, challenge, climax, and resolution. Divide students into groups. Have each group write a script for a cartoon and create its cartoon story. Then, have each group upload its cartoon to ToonTube to share it with others.

> Have students each create their own cartoon stories. Then, have them share their stories with their parents and classmates during an open house night.

At Home

> Work with your child to create an engaging story for his or her cartoon. Recruit additional family members to speak the parts of different characters. Practice your speaking parts before recording.

> Help your child adapt a scene from his or her favorite movie or TV show to become a cartoon.

GarageBand

Apple

Suggested Grades
K–12

Available
iTunes

Description

Let your child's musical creativity soar with the *GarageBand* app. Explore different instruments and sounds. Create multi-track songs and record your own vocals. *GarageBand* provides the power to create music anywhere. *GarageBand* includes the following key features:

> Multiple instruments, including guitars, keyboard, and drums

> Record function

> Sampler to record new sounds to use with onscreen keyboard

> Mixing board to create and edit up to eight instrumental and vocal tracks

> Option to export music tracks to *GarageBand* for Mac or email.

At School

> Teach students the basic functions of the *GarageBand* app. Then, place this app in a center and allow students to experiment with the different instruments.

> In teacher-led small groups, have students describe each instrument. Then, have each student choose an instrument and create an instrument track.

> With younger students, display real instruments if available, for students to explore. Allow students to experiment playing with the real instruments and the virtual instruments in *GarageBand*. Then, lead a discussion with students about how the real instruments compare to the virtual instruments.

> Have older students work in pairs. Instruct students to work together to create an original piece of music to complement a writing activity they have recently completed. Have them discuss what instruments they will use and what tone they want to set with their musical score. Then, have them read their text set to the music.

At Home

> Walk your child through the different functions that *GarageBand* offers. Talk to your child about the different elements that go into a single piece of music.

> Create pieces of music with your child. Ask your child what types of instruments he or she would like to use and which they think will sound best and why.

    © Shell Education

Dragon Dictation

Nuance Communications

Suggested Grades
K–12

Available
iTunes

Description

Use the power of *Dragon Dictation* to record your thoughts directly to text. You speak, it types. This productivity app helps you get your ideas onto the page for faster organization. *Dragon Dictation* includes the following key features:

> Speech-to-text functionality

> Editing capability directly in app

> Correction, formatting, and punctuation commands

> Sharing via email and social networks

At School

> In a whole-group instructional setting, connect your mobile device to a projector. Show students the different functions of *Dragon Dictation* and how to record and talk into the mobile device's microphone. Then, show students how to edit their work within the application. Have students write sentences related to a recent grammar lesson, and ask for volunteers to dictate them to the application. Edit the sentences as a class.

> In pairs, instruct students to dictate a recent writing assignment. Have each pair work together to edit and then email the writing assignment to you.

> Place this app in a center and allow students to narrate a story or personal narrative. Have them edit and revise their dictation and then email it to you.

At Home

> Have your child tell a story while you use *Dragon Dictation* to capture it. Read the dictation recorded by *Dragon Dictation* and discuss whether any editing needs to be done.

> Take turns creating silly sentences with your child and then reading them back in the app. Share your silly sentences with another family member.

> Work with your child to dictate a school essay. Then, have your child export the essay to a computer, and help him or her complete the publishing process.

Popplet

Notion, Inc.

Suggested Grades
K–12

Available
iTunes

Description

Map out your thoughts, brainstorm, and collaborate with the easy-to-use *Popplet* app. This app allows you to organize and revise your ideas. *Popplet* includes the following key features:

> Color-adjustable brainstorm bubbles

> Text, drawing, and photo integration

> Real-time Internet collaboration

> Exporting to mobile device's photo gallery or email

At School

> Prior to whole-group instruction, create different types of basic graphic organizers to share with students. Connect your mobile device to a projector. Display the *Popplet* app and show students the different types of graphic organizers. Facilitate a general discussion about the best ways to organize information into popplets and graphic organizers.

> In small groups, have students brainstorm ideas for a writing assignment. Have students work together (using the collaboration feature, if possible) to create a comprehensive graphic organizer. Then, have them use their graphic organizer to compose their writing assignment.

> Have younger students make a popplet using only pictures that they draw. Then, help them label each image with a caption.

At Home

> Show your child how to use the *Popplet* app. Then, help him or her to make a family tree popplet. Have your child tell you who should be included in the family tree. Take pictures or use existing pictures of each family member in your popplet. Email the family tree to your family when it is complete.

> Ask your child about his or her day. Then, have your child create a sequence-of-events popplet that shows what he or she they did during the day. Work with your child to map out each event sequentially. Discuss your child's completed popplet.

© Shell Education

ScreenChomp

TechSmith Corporation

Suggested Grades
4–12

Available
iTunes

Description

ScreenChomp uses a simple virtual whiteboard canvas and allows you to record important parts of lessons, as well as quick tutorials and screencasts. This learning tool can be used to teach as well as to learn and study. *ScreenChomp* includes the following key features:

> Virtual whiteboard with markers

> Record function

> Photo integration

> Sharing to **www.screenchomp.com**, Facebook, and Twitter

> Exporting to MPEG-4

At School

> In pairs, have students create a screenchomp that reviews a recent standard that was taught. For example, students may create a screenchomp that explains how to find the greatest common factor of two numbers. Or, they may create a screenchomp of how to find Australia or another country on a map. Have them plan out how they will explain the standard they have chosen before they record their screenchomp.

> In a whole-group instructional setting, connect your mobile device to a projector. Use *ScreenChomp* as an interactive whiteboard to record the guided practice portion of a lesson. Save the screenchomp created and allow students to review the video, as necessary. Upload your screenchomp to **www.screenchomp.com** for others to benefit, if desired.

At Home

> Have your child choose something that he or she enjoys or feels skilled at doing. Then, have him or her create a screenchomp that explains how to do that particular activity.

> Help your child study by creating screenchomps for concepts that he or she finds difficult. Have your child refer to the screenchomps you have created for reference.

360 Panorama

Occipital

Suggested Grades
3–12

Available
iTunes, Google Play

Description

Take a complete 360-degree panoramic picture anywhere you can take your mobile device. Share a 360-degree view of your favorite places with your family, friends, students, and teachers. *360 Panorama* includes the following key features:

> 360-degree-panorama camera function

> Caption text box

> Sharing to computer, email, and social networking sites

At School

> Take 360-degree panorama pictures of different places around school. Then, place this app in a center and have students write a short description paragraph of what they see in one of the panoramas.

> In pairs, have students take a mobile device to their favorite place on the playground. Then, have them take turns taking 360-degree panoramas that include their partners. Have pairs present and describe their panoramas to the class by connecting the mobile device to a projector.

> Take *360 Panorama* on a class field trip and distribute mobile device(s) to students throughout the day. When you return to the classroom, organize the panoramas and have students review their trip. Then, have students write a summary of their field trip.

At Home

> Take 360-degree panoramas around town at your child's favorite places. Have your child describe what is shown in each panorama. Then, discuss what your child enjoys about each place.

> Use the panoramas you and your child have taken to play a game of scavenger hunt. Ask your child to find certain objects or people in the panorama.

> Have your child take a 360-degree panorama of a favorite room in the house, and have him or her share the panorama in a show-and-tell fashion.

iMovie

Apple

Suggested Grades
4–12

Available
iTunes

Description

Create polished movies and photo slide shows using *iMovie's* simple and intuitive interface anytime, anywhere. Add photos and movies, choose transitions and themes, and add music all in a matter of minutes. *iMovie* includes the following key features:

> Multi-touch functionality, including tap to add photos, videos, and music

> Video editing directly from mobile device

> Recording and editing functionality for soundtrack or narrative

> Publishing to social networking sites, email, mobile device's camera roll, and more

At School

> Divide the class into small groups and lead students to a predetermined area of the school campus. Instruct students to work in groups to create a documentary-style video that relates to something that they have learned about in class. Once groups have completed their videos, have them share their videos with the class.

> Distribute the mobile device to different students throughout the day in class or on a field trip. Have students take pictures and video clips of their classmates. Then, in a whole-group instructional setting, connect your mobile device to a projector. As a class, choose photos and video clips to create a simple video. Add theme music or sound effects. Then, discuss whether the video accurately depicts the day's events.

> In pairs, have students create a mock interview or newscast using *iMovie*. Then, have them share their videos with the class.

At Home

> Have your child use family photos to create a family scrapbook video. Help your child narrate the video to explain what is going on in each picture.

> Ask your child about his or her hobbies. Then, help your child create a video explaining how they participate in the hobbies and why the hobbies are important.

> Have your child create a video while on a family trip to document and narrate what happens each day, as if he or she were a part of a reality-TV show. Also, have your child interview family members about their favorite parts of the trip.

MaxJournal

Omaxmedia

Suggested Grades
4–12

Available
iTunes

Description

Document your thoughts, make a list, take notes, or keep a daily journal. Whatever your journaling needs, *MaxJournal* has you covered. This easy to use journaling app keeps your entries organized by date and secures them with password protection. *MaxJournal* includes the following key features:

> Various font styles and sizes

> Multiple journal creation

> Photos and images can attach to entries

> Password protection

> Exports journals to PDF and email

At School

> In a whole-group instructional setting, connect your mobile device to a projector. Explain or review the various elements of a journal entry. Then, demonstrate the features of the *MaxJournal* app with students. As a class, discuss the various reasons that people may keep a journal.

> Place this app in a center and allow students to create their own journal. Be sure to have them password protect their journal, so other students cannot read what they have written. Have students keep a weekly journal and email you a copy of their journal entry if they feel comfortable.

> Give students a writing prompt so that they may write a journal entry. Have students add images to their entries. Then, have students export their entries to a class computer or email them to you.

At Home

> Have your child create a daily journal to reflect on what he or she has learned, what challenges he or she has faced, and the victories he or she has experienced.

> Work with your child to create a travel or hobby journal to keep a daily log while traveling or as he or she continues the hobby. Encourage your child to share his or her thoughts with you.

© Shell Education

Strip Designer

Vivid Apps

Suggested Grades
4–12

Available
iTunes

Description

Use your mobile device to turn photos into humorous, interesting, or action-packed comic strips. Have you ever dreamed of being a superhero? With *Strip Designer*, you can be the superhero of your own comic strips. *Strip Designer* includes the following key features:

> Over 100 comic strip templates with multiple text balloons, stickers, color gradients and cell styles to choose from

> Importing photos from your own photo library

> Option to export comic strips to PDF

> Auto-save

At School

> In a whole-group instructional setting, connect your mobile device to a projector. Go over all of the functions present in the *Strip Designer*. Take photos of a few students working, and then create a simple comic strip as a class.

> In a small group, explain to students that they will be creating a comic strip. Have students create an original dialogue or short screenplay, and then have them create a storyboard comic strip that depicts it. Allow students time to take photos to include in their comic strips. Have students present their comic strips to the class.

> In pairs, assign students a science or math concept that they can explain in a comic strip. Encourage them to include and create a superhero that can help explain the assigned concept. Have students take pictures and create original art to include in their comic strips. Then, have students export their comic strips to a PDF file.

At Home

> Discuss a fun family event or fond family memory with your child. Have him or her create a comic strip that captures those memories. Use family photos and original drawings to complete the comic strip. Then, share the comic strip with your family.

> Encourage your child to create a superhero and design a comic strip to tell the story of the superhero. Help them design the superhero's outfit, the plot, and the settings that will be used in the comic. Then, work together to create the comic strip.

GoodReader

Good.iWare Ltd.

Suggested Grades
4–12

Available
iTunes

Description

GoodReader allows the freedom to take notes directly on popular file formats. Highlight important passages. Write notes on student work and email feedback. Send homework to students that can be completed digitally. *GoodReader* includes the following key features:

> Reads multiple file types, including .pdf, .txt, .doc, .xls, and .ppt

> Annotation tools such as Highlighter, Text Box, and Shapes

> Save feature

> Folders for file organization

> Sharing via WiFi or USB to computer, email, Dropbox, and Google Docs™

At School

> In a whole-group instructional setting, connect your mobile device to a projector. Demonstrate how to take notes to increase reading comprehension. Show students how to use the Highlighter and Text Box tools to leave notes about the important elements within a text. Then, give students a new piece of text and ask for volunteers to help you annotate it.

> Place this app in a center or workstation, and provide students with an activity sheet file already loaded. Have students annotate the activity sheet to complete it and save a copy of the file with their name. Then, have them email the file to you.

> Have students save a current writing activity as a PDF file and email it to you. Then, review and edit their writing and email it back to students for revision.

At Home

> Load a PDF version of your child's favorite storybook to *GoodReader* and have your child bookmark his or her favorite page. Work with your child to highlight, circle, or note different parts of speech or key vocabulary that can be found in the text. Have your child type an alternate ending in a text box or pop-up note.

> Send PDF versions of family pictures to *GoodReader*. Have your child create captions for each picture using text boxes. Then, email the pictures to your family.

© Shell Education

Index